Successful
SAUDI ARABIAN WOMEN:
THEIR GEMS OF WISDOM

CREATIVE

Creative Associates Publishers

Creative Associates International, Inc.
5301 Wisconsin Ave., NW, Suite 700
Washington, DC 20015
Email: CREATIVE@CREATIVEDC.COM
Phone (202) 966-5804 * Fax (202) 363-4771

www.CREATIVEASSOCIATESINTERNATIONAL.com

Freeman, Sharon T. and Kruvant, M. Charito

Successful Saudi Arabian Women: Their Gems of Wisdom

Sharon T. Freeman, Ph.D. and Kruvant, M. Charito

ISBN 978-0-9962688-0-6

Women Leaders
Women & Economic Empowerment
Women & Culture
Muslim Women
Muslim Women in Saudi Arabia

I. Freeman, Sharon T. and Kruvant, M. Charito   II. Title.

ISBN 978-0-9962688-0-6 (Trade Paper)

Publisher:

Creative Associates Publishers

Creative Associates International, Inc.

5301 Wisconsin Ave., NW, Suite 700
Washington, DC 20015
Email: CREATIVE@CREATIVEDC.COM
www.CREATIVE ASSOCIATESINTERNATIONAL.com
Phone (202) 966-5804 * Fax (202) 363-4771

Cover design and Graphic layout by Creative Services, Chester, Maryland

Successful Saudi Arabian Women: Their Gems of Wisdom

Table of Contents

Welcome Message

E ducation is one of the key foundations for greatness. History shows that those who are educated dream bigger dreams and increase their chances of making their dreams come true with the tools and knowledge they acquire through education.

History is also a witness to the many contributions that educated women have made to the greatness of their societies and to the happiness and well-being of their immediate families and broader communities.

M. Charito Kruvant

In the complex world in which we are living in the 21st century, no one knows the answers about what's going to happen tomorrow or how to create the change and progress that we desire as human beings, but we do know one thing for sure: Knowledge is power; the more we know the better off we will be in navigating the future.

We also know that among the prosperous nations in the world, Saudi Arabia has demonstrated its embrace of education in the most profound and meaningful way. It has made enormous investments in educating her people and many Saudi women have been among the beneficiaries of this vison, commitment, and investment. The stories of the women in this book prove that the investment in education is paying off. These women are not just educated for education's sake; they are using their education in ways that are lifting the society up higher and higher.

The importance of education and its transformative potential is not news to Creative. For the past 40 years Creative has been at the forefront of training education professionals and helping nations develop education curricula. At the same time, we have helped ensure that women around the world take advantage of the opportunity to become educated and to leverage their education for the good of the societies in which they live.

We are very pleased to have had this opportunity to come to know some of Saudi Arabia's leading professional women and to share information about their accomplishments with our readers. There has been too much distance between these women and many of their sisters around the world and we hope that this book brings all of us closer together. After all, we are all human and want the same things for our children, families, and countries. We want to be happy and fulfilled and we believe that women who are educated have a chance to apply their education in ways that make everybody better off, including themselves.

I hope that you enjoy learning more about the powerful impact education has had in these successful women's lives.

Peace,
Charito

CREATIVE

About Creative

Creative Associates International is a pioneering women-owned and managed professional and technical services firm that provides on-the-ground services around the world to promote international development and accelerate the pace of economic growth and sustainability.

As a woman-owned firm that was established in 1977 by four enterprising women, the founders of the company know what it takes for women to excel and to soar professionally. It takes, courage, stamina, intellect, and a commitment to values, and beliefs; importantly, it takes a desire to make a positive contribution in the world.

The women featured in this book have shown the same spirit and dedication to their work. For Creative, its core values and professionalism have been a guiding beacon in its work that has focused on education, economic growth, youth, workforce development, governance and elections, and other key areas since 1977. As a result, Creative Associates International has become one of the leading development practitioner companies in the U.S.

As a leader in the field of international development, Creative works in partnership with multi-faith communities and networks of local, regional and national non-governmental organizations, international donors, multilateral organizations, and universities across the globe. In all of its endeavors, Creative has worked particularly close with women who are at once the beneficiaries of Creative's services, the providers of service, and those who inform best practices and apply the latest thinking to accomplishing the goals we seek in our work.

It has been Creative's experience that if you really want to find the *"Gems of Wisdom"* in any situation, talk to the women.

This book is a part of our ongoing efforts, which began 40 years ago, to listen to, engage, connect with, and understand women in order to glean deeper insights into societies and to take advantage of their wealth of knowledge that we consider *"Gems of Wisdom."*

Today, with active programs in more than 20 countries, with a professional staff of nearly 1,000 people around the world, and a history of having worked in more than 85 countries, we have realized one of the important things to do in the world to get ahead is to listen to the women. ❧

About Co-Author

M. Charito Kruvant

Charito was born in Bolivia at a time when the prospects for women to realize their full potential was severely limited, not just in Bolivia, but all over the world. How could Charito have imagined that one day she would rise up and not only realize her potential but help women around the world do the same?

What she has achieved in business, establishing and directing Creative Associates International, a company that has annual revenues of approximately $200 million, is indeed unimaginable not just in hindsight but even in today's terms, and by every measure. What made the critical difference for Charito was understanding very early on that the only way to realize one's potential is by being educated. Charito studied education as a discipline and then leveraged her knowledge to help women around the world become educated and to understand that education was the key to their futures.

Over the period of the last forty years, Creative Associates International, which Charito co-founded with three other enterprising women partners, has demonstrated that education is an essential and necessary ingredient for economic development and a prerequisite for women to become major contributors to their families, communities, and societies.

Just as the success of the women in this book can be attributed in part to their high levels of educational attainment, Charito has seen the same phenomenon the world over. When she looks back on her native Bolivia, for instance, she can see that whereas few girls were educated when she was a child, today nearly all (93.6%) girls over the age of 15 are literate. When she looks back at her second home, Argentina, where she obtained her first university degree, she can look with pride at the fact that a woman has risen to become the President of the country and that educational attainment for girls over the age of 10 stands at over 98 percent.

When Charito looks at the trail that Creative Associates has blazed as a leading global educational development firm, she also sees many success stories, and can confidently conclude that the pioneering work of the firm in developing and delivering state-of-the-art early grade reading materials and curriculum development approaches has had a significant and lasting impact. Creative's work in education has contributed to the advancement of the education systems in the 80 countries in which the firm has worked.

Never content to sit back and rest, Charito and the firm she leads continue to make new strides and work in areas where others dare not, where only a firm of Creative's stature is prepared to take on new challenges in education, conflict mitigation and conceiving new ideas to bring about peace and prosperity in the world.

Charito is particularly happy to take this moment to share the stories of Saudi women because she recognizes that Saudi Arabia is a leader and that Saudi women are inspiring examples of harnessing education to realize their full potential. The women profiled here stand as a powerful example to others in the Middle East and to Muslim societies. The message from the women is clear and consistent with Charito's own: educated women are equipped to make significant contributions to society and the sky is the limit on what those contributions might be in the future. ❧

About Co-Author

Dr. Sharon T. Freeman

Dr. Freeman has a four decades long distinguished career in the field of international development and formerly lived and worked in Hong Kong for 12 years. She is also entrepreneur, international development and trade expert, and the writer and publisher of 20 books on topics including how to export and import and how to work with the U.S. Government; she has also written books on such topical issues as women leadership and entrepreneurship, political leadership, youth leadership, and on how individuals and societies are "going green," as well as about China in Africa, among other topics. Dr. Freeman and co-author Charito Kruvant have been a writing team for over ten years and have jointly written and published four books previously.

Dr. Freeman has worked in over 100 countries throughout her career, including extensively in the Middle East. In the late 1970s, for instance, she was a pioneer in working with Booz, Allen & Hamilton on planning the management plan for the building of two new cities in Saudi Arabia at the time: Jubail and Yanbu. Years later, Dr. Freeman returned to Saudi Arabia to give lectures to women on small business development. She similarly worked in Bahrain, and spent considerable time working in Sharjah, U.A.E., where she helped to plan the Sharjah Free Trade Zone.

She currently serves as an appointed Advisor on trade to the U.S. Secretary of Commerce and to the U.S. Trade Representative. She formerly also advised the U.S. Export-Import Bank, the Small Business Administration, and the U.S. Department on Energy on how to increase the participation of minorities and women in their procurements. Dr. Freeman has been awarded many honors in recognition of her work as an advocate for the enfranchisement of women and minorities.

For the past four years, Dr. Freeman has joined forces with Creative Associates International where she continues her writing and publishing with the co-author and where she serves as a Director and Analyst.

Dr. Freeman received two undergraduate degrees from Carnegie-Mellon and a Master's of Science in Public Policy and Management from Carnegie-Mellon as well. Her Ph.D. in Applied Management & Decision Sciences was conferred by Walden University. ❧

Acknowledgments

First and foremost, we would like to thank and acknowledge the women featured in this book who have taken the time out of their busy schedules to share their stories with the readers. In so doing, their goal is to shed light on the common threads that bind us as human beings, as concerned citizens, and as family and community members. Their stories demonstrate their vast capabilities, their eagerness to make a positive contribution to their societies, and their successes in so doing.

Importantly, we also acknowledge and express our gratitude to the leadership of the Academic Company for Educational Service (ACES) and its staff for fully supporting this undertaking by selecting the women who are profiled and for providing valuable insights into the culture of the society. We also wish to thank our Creative Associates Saudi-based representative, Sonia Shahin, who supported and promoted this project in every way.

Readers should walk away with a richer understanding of Saudi culture and the strides that are being made by women today. Their successes are proof positive that education is a key contributing factor for unharnessing and unleashing the inner greatness of these women across a broad spectrum of professional endeavors.

To paraphrase one of the women in the book, Professor Dr. Selwa Al-Hazzaa, Member of the Shura Council, "…one grain of sand is uncountable in its aggregation, but one tiny grain of sand can bring to a screeching halt the most highly sophisticated jet engine." The professional women of Saudi Arabia are like tiny grains of sand that are so important and so potentially impactful, yet they happily coexist in their families and communities in the aggregate. But, when they are singled out and given a chance to show what they can do, it's plain for all to see just how much one tiny grain can matter.

M. Charito Kruvant and Sharon T. Freeman, Ph.D.

Introduction

I n this one–of-a-kind series of intimate first-person stories about successful Saudi Arabian professional women, readers can peek behind the veil to view a snapshot of what it took for them to get to where they are. This is unprecedented. Internet searches about these women yield information about the awards they have won but not about how they feel about their successes or what it took to achieve them.

Through their stories the women paint portraits in soft hues that delicately shine a light on Saudi society and their role in it. The women featured are doctors, lawyers, inventors, advocates, wives, and mothers—and more, who in their respective capacities have made major contributors to their professions and to society. Their professional accomplishments and proficiency in multitasking suggest that the potential of women is far greater than has been realized. However, this is contrasted with the reality of the boundaries imposed on them as first generation professional women in a traditional society. For now, such women are on a proving ground; they must demonstrate that they can accomplish great things professionally while also holding fast to the values and expectations of societies, and while performing the traditional duties of a Muslim woman. The proof that their experience and performance is providing is gradually and steadily laying the foundation for expanded possibilities for women in the future.

Being a trailblazer is not easy for anyone in any society but, arguably, it might just be a little bit harder for Saudi women. Somehow they have managed to break through and the question is: How did they do that?

From the evidence that their stories provide, there are four essential elements of success: being highly educated, being socially acceptable, being fortunate in the timing of their birth, and most importantly, having had fathers and husbands who enabled and supported their success.

The positive role their fathers played in their lives is particularly notable because girls must have their permission to seek education and their encouragement to leverage it for professional purposes. This is significant because education is the only proven pathway to professional success for women in Saudi Arabia.

Fathers have unmatched power to encourage and sanction their daughters' aspirations beyond merely leading a domestic life and, on the flip side, they also have the power to curtail aspirations at an early age. Husbands too possess the power to add fuel to the fire or to extinguish it. Thus first, the girl must aspire to be successful and to become educated; next, the father must sanction her dreams, and finally, the husband must permit those dreams to be realized.

At the heart of the equation is the girl herself. How does she become inspired to aspire?

Most of the women profiled here had access to only tiny bits of information during their childhood, which came mostly from books their mothers typically could not read. Those little nuggets fired up their imaginations and, like coals in a fire, their dreams burned brightly. Visions of a future brighter than the fate of most females in their immediate family and environments shone before them.

Making their dreams come true wasn't easy, however. Being the first in their family to study a particular discipline or to study in the west, as most in this book did, was challenging. They had to master the English language and study long and hard for many years to get where they are today. While they were studying, most also had multiple children and had to figure out how to effectively navigate new societies in the west while holding true to their customs and religion.

It is important to understand that success for women in Saudi Arabia always has two dimensions: professional and personal. Professionally, Saudi women are expected to obtain the highest level of academic credentials possible and then draw on their network to get a job that permits them to productively apply that knowledge. Personal success encompasses much more, requiring Saudi women to walk a thin line between being different – because of their high level of education – while also fitting in because of their adherence to shared values and customs.

The latter is what makes this book a breakthrough. Saudi professional women have mastered how to fit in. Therefore, stepping out to tell their individual personal stories is a big step and one they have taken with a degree of caution and apprehension.

In Saudi Arabia, family is the most important social institution. It is the primary basis of identity and status, and the immediate focus of individual loyalty. A successful Saudi woman is one whose personal and professional aspirations are sanctioned and approved by her family. Because the possession of academic credentials alone is insufficient for conferring high social status, there is a limit to the degree to which women are willing to be outliers in order to be "professionally successful." Saudi women must, above all, successfully navigate society and be accepted by society.

Saudi society values behavior that displays generosity, selflessness and hospitality. Importantly, it values deference to hierarchy in the family, mastery over one's emotions, as well as a willingness to support other family members and assume responsibility for their errors.

Two main themes appear throughout the stories of the women in this book: acceptance and navigation. To make it in this world, these women had to accept that which society was not ready to change: arranged marriages, covering up, seeking permission from their fathers or husbands at every turn and having limited mobility. These same women spotted and seized opportunities outside of traditional expectations, making them captains of their own destiny, which is and where navigation comes in.

The women in this book embraced educational opportunity, but luck also played an important role. They were lucky enough to have the support of their fathers and husbands. Timing was also important. They all received scholarships at a time when that narrow window of opportunity was beginning to open.

Their mothers didn't have that window. Most of the women in this book have mothers who are only about a decade and a half older than themselves who were customarily forced to be illiterate.

If this were a book about "unsuccessful" Saudi Arabian women we might read one story after another of women who never got out of the gate, those that never had a chance. But, that's another book. Unabashedly, this is a book about the "glass being half full." It presents small insights into the hearts and stories of Saudi Arabian women who made it based on their education, acumen and personal navigation of the society. One thing about their "half full glasses:" they had to "dance" without spilling its contents.

The "break out" stories revealed in this book illustrate the gigantic leap women have taken in Saudi Arabia in the past few decades when, not long before, it was frowned upon (or worse) even to mention the whole name of a female in public. These women have placed themselves in the spotlight to tell their stories, *to whatever degree of frankness*, which is a very big step of self-assertion. While the entirety of their back stories aren't necessarily revealed, we're grateful for the insights and, indeed, for the gems of wisdom they have shared.

It is not possible to fully appreciate the stories in this book without understanding the societal and cultural context in which they have occurred. For instance, when a woman says, "I am grateful to my husband for his support," that is more than a casual statement because a husband *must* give his support for what his wife is doing or it is unlikely she would be permitted to do it. Acts considered to be routine in other countries such as leaving the house, visiting other cities, regions, or countries, working alongside men and even being employed require the husband's permission in Saudi Arabia. Thus, as we applaud the women in this book for their accomplishments, we must also applaud their fathers and spouses who both allowed and encouraged them.

The key when reading these stories is to be mindful of time. If a woman was born in the 1950s, that means one thing in terms of the information she had at her disposal and about the prevailing norms and attitudes of that time; if she was born in the 1960s, it was different, and so on.

What were the barriers each woman profiled had to overcome given the period in which she came of age? This is a question that cannot be fully be answered in the confines of this book, for some barriers are undoubtedly internal to the person and her family, while others are externally imposed. What we know for certain is that every move the woman makes has circles of influence and consent around it, with one sphere inside another, and another, and another.

Societal change, especially as it relates to women within Saudi Arabia, entails a process of "bringing up the rear." Accordingly, acceptance of societal change occurs at different rates within the society, typically from the front to the back rather than the other way around. At the "front" are the enlightened ones, the broadly educated people and at the "rear" are those who are not. The latter group is composed of both women and men who were born at a time and in a place that did not permit them to be educated in ways other than how they were educated, if they were educated at all.

Today's Saudi Arabia stands with one foot firmly placed among the most highly developed nations of the world with the other lagging behind. It still has a substantial population that lives in rural areas distant from developed urban centers, with some living as nomadic and semi-nomadic herdsmen and others as oasis agricultural workers. Well into the 20th century, several great deserts cut tribal groups off from one another and isolated Najd from other areas of the country, resulting in a high degree of cultural and religious homogeneity among the inhabitants. The majority follow Sunni Wahhabi Islam and embrace a patriarchal family system. While the desert can be more easily traversed today, the great gulf between conservative and liberal viewpoints remains far apart.

Saudi Arabia's population continues to present a picture of cultural contrasts. On the one hand, Saudi people feel a strong desire to live one's life according to God's laws as revealed through the Holy Quran and the life of the Prophet Muhammad. At the same time, the interpretation of what it means to live according to God's laws has assumed different meanings to different groups of people: some wish to adjust traditional values to the circumstances of the present while others wish to adjust the circumstances of the present to traditional values. In no aspect of Saudi society is this tension more manifest than in the question of the role of women. The conservative view favors complete separation of women from men in public life, with the education of women devoted to domestic skills, whereas the liberal view has sought to transform "separation values" into "modesty values," allowing the expansion of women's opportunities in work and education.

As the debate rages on, the women in this book quietly and cleverly seized educational opportunities, laying the foundation to become indispensable to Saudi society by virtue of the knowledge and unique skills they possess.

Saudi society is complex, rich in both history and culture, and imbued with certain social contracts. The following offers a brief overview of Saudi Arabia's history, culture, and some of the social contracts.

3,000 Year Historical Timeline of Saudi Arabia: At a Glance

For a thousand years BC, and for another thousand and a half years thereafter, nomadic lifestyles and trade dominated the culture and economy of what has become Saudi Arabia. The Bedouins of the area that stretched from the vast deserts of North Africa to the rocky sands of the Middle East are semi-nomadic. Territory was traditionally divided into tribes or clans. From their original home in the Arabian Peninsula, the Bedouins spread out to surrounding deserts, forced out by the lack of water and food. Historically, the Bedouin engaged in nomadic herding, agriculture and occasional fishing. A major source of income was taxation of caravans and tributes collected from non-Bedouin settlements. They also earned income by transporting goods and people in caravans across the desert. Scarcity of water and having no permanent pastoral land required them to move constantly.

Prophet Muhammad, Prophet of Islam

In 570 CE things changed with the birth of Prophet Muhammad, Prophet of Islam. According to Muslim tradition, Prophet Muhammad succeeded in converting most of the Bedouin to Islam before he died.

A thousand years later, in the 15th century, the Saud dynasty was founded in the region around today's Riyadh. Around 300 years later in the mid-18th century, Muhammad ibn Abd al-Wahhab, religious leader, established a sect of Islam that was supported by the Saud dynasty. This movement soon established a national state in Najd, the center of Arabia.

In 1802, Mecca was conquered by the Wahhabis, but by 1812 they were driven out. In 1818, Wahhbis and Saudis founded their capital in Riyadh, but in 1865 civil war broke out and the dynasty fell apart. Arabia was divided between different clans and the Ottomans. By the 20th century the Wahhbis and Saudis were in charge again and the modern history of Saudi Arabia began.

20th & 21st Century Saudi Arabia: At A Glance[1]

1902: King Abdul Aziz Ibn Saud (1876-1953) retakes Riyadh and in 1906 took control over Najd. This conquest, referred to as a "Jihad" campaign, unified the scattered parts and splintered tribes of the Arabian Peninsula under the banner: *"There is no god but Allah and Mohammed is the Messenger of Allah."*

1926: Abdul Aziz declares himself King of Hijaz. Notably, in the years from 1924 Abdul Aziz broke with the Wahhabis and allowed the introduction of modern inventions, things that the Wahhabis looked upon as un-Islamic.

1932: Conquered territories are unified and named Saudi Arabia and Abdul Aziz takes the name "King of Saudi Arabia."

1938: Oil is discovered and the next year oil exploitation commenced. During this time Abdul Aziz started a large-scale modernization program, which included the establishment of several ministries and diplomatic relations in accordance with officially recognized political representation, including the appointment of ambassadors.

1951: An agreement with Aramco (Arabian American Oil Company) gives Saudi Arabia 50% of all earnings from the oil and Aramco starts paying tax to Saudi Arabia instead of to the U.S. Government.

1953: King Abdul Aziz died in 1953 and was succeeded by his son Saud.

1958: The constitution was changed and the absolute power of kings was reduced. Legislative and executive powers were transferred to the prime minister and a cabinet system was introduced.

1960: Saudi Arabia participated in the formation of OPEC to help sustain international oil prices.

---

[1] Summarized from: The Saudi Network, http://the-saudi.net/saudi-arabia/saudi_history.htm (accessed, March, 2015)

1962: King Saud is forced to transfer effective power to his brother Faisal due to criticisms of Saud's lack of control over economy.

1964: Prince Faisal replaced Saud as king; the political system he established is still in use today.

Faisal's reign initiated a massive education program. Expenditures for education increased to an annual level of approximately 10 percent of the budget. Vocational training centers and institutes of higher education were built in addition to the more than 125 elementary and secondary schools built annually. Women's demands, increasingly vocalized, led to the establishment of elementary schools for girls. These schools were placed under religious control to pacify those who were opposed to education for women. Health centers also multiplied.

1974: Saudi Arabia takes over more of the control over Aramco and revenues increase greatly.

1975: King Faisal is murdered and Khalid becomes the new king but due to his weak health his brother Fahd was effectively in charge.

1979 (November 20): The Grand Mosque of Mecca was taken over by a group of armed men who wanted the Saud family to step down in order to return to the original ways of Islam. This entailed, among other things, a repudiation of the west; an end of education of women, abolition of television and expulsion of non-Muslims. It was proclaimed that "the ruling Al Saud dynasty had lost its legitimacy because it was corrupt, ostentatious and had destroyed Saudi culture by an aggressive policy of westernization."

This was a bell weather moment in the history of Saudi Arabia. As a result, many things changed. Specifically, in the aftermath, Saudi King Khaled gave the ulama and religious conservatives more power over the next decade. He is thought to have believed that "the solution to the religious upheaval was simple -- more religion." First, photographs of women in newspapers were banned, then women on television. Cinemas and music shops were shut down. School curricula were changed to provide more hours of religious studies. Importantly, gender segregation was extended "to the humblest coffee shop," and the religious police became more assertive.

1982: King Khalid dies and is succeeded by King Fahd.

1990: The Iraqi invasion of Kuwait was dramatic to Saudi politics and security. Saudi Arabia allowed hundreds of thousands of foreign troops (mainly U.S.) to be stationed on their own soil.

1992: Constitutional changes, where a consultative council, Shura, is established, along with a bill of rights, and the rules of succession for the King.

2000-January 2015: King Abdullah's Reign: His reign ushered in many reforms, including many that favored women.

> He realized a top-to-bottom restructuring of the country's courts to introduce, among other things, review of judicial decisions and more professional training for Shari'a judges. He developed a new investment promotion agency to overhaul the once-convoluted process of starting a business in Saudi Arabia. He created a regulatory body for capital markets. He has promoted the construction of the King Abdullah University for Science and Technology (the country's new flagship and controversially co-ed institution for advanced scientific research). He invested in educating the workforce for future jobs and encouraged the development of non-hydrocarbon sectors. The Kingdom's 2010 budget reflected these priorities—about 25 percent was devoted to education alone.

> King Abdullah worked to incorporate women into Saudi politics; in September 2011, he signed a royal decree granting women the right to vote and run in the next municipal election, and in January 2013, he appointed thirty women to the 150-member Shura Council.

January 2015-: Salman bin Abdulaziz Al Saud was crowned as the new King of Saudi Arabia on 23 January 2015 following the death of his half-brother, King Abdullah.

Note that key milestones for women in the timeline include the mid-1960s, when King Faisal promoted public education and established elementary schools for girls; 1979, when things clamped down for females; and finally, in the 21st century, when it swung back in a positive direction for women during the reign of King Abdullah. All together, this is not a lot of time but within these narrow windows of opportunity, the women in this book emerged and ascended to the highest levels possible in their time. Their successes underscore the importance of education and its potential to transform the lives of individuals and families, as well as the destinies of communities and nations.

Insights into Saudi Arabian Culture and Traditions

Information to help demystify Saudi Arabia and to provide context for the women's stories in the book is provided below. The primary source of this information is the U.S. Library of Congress publication, *Saudi: Arabia: A Country Study (1993)*. It was selected as the main reference because it is well-researched and considered to be one of the most comprehensive and authoritative sources that is available in English. The questions posed below are the author's and the answers are taken from the Library of Congress country study, and from other sources where indicated.

Wahhabi Theology

What is Wahhbi Islam and how did it become entrenched in Saudi Arabia?

Wahhbi Islam is a religious movement or offshoot of Sunni Islam. It has been variously described as "orthodox, ultraconservative, austere, fundamentalist, or puritanical;" it came into being as an Islamic "reform movement" to restore "pure monotheistic worship." It began in central Arabia in the mid-eighteenth century and grew out of the scholarship and preaching of Muhammad ibn Abd al Wahhab, a scholar of Islamic jurisprudence who had studied in Mesopotamia and the Hijaz before returning to his native Najd to preach his message of Islamic reform.[2]

Muhammad ibn Abd al Wahhab was concerned with the way the people of Najd engaged in practices he considered polytheistic, such as praying to saints; making pilgrimages to tombs and special mosques; venerating trees, caves, and stones; and using votive and sacrificial offerings. He was also concerned by what he viewed as a laxity in adhering to Islamic law and in performing religious devotions, such as indifference to the plight of widows and orphans, adultery, lack of attention to obligatory prayers, and failure to allocate shares of inheritance fairly to women. When he began to preach against these breaches of Islamic laws, he characterized customary practices as *jahiliya*, the same term used to describe the ignorance of Arabians before the Prophet. Initially, his preaching encountered opposition, but he eventually came under the protection of a local chieftain named Muhammad ibn Saud, with whom he formed an alliance.

[2] http://en.wikipedia.org/wiki/Wahhabism (Accessed April 2015)

The endurance of the Wahhabi movement's influence may be attributed to the close association between the founder of the movement and the politically powerful Al Saud in southern Najd. This association between the Al Saud and the Al ash Shaykh, as Muhammad ibn Abd al Wahhab and his descendants came to be known, effectively converted political loyalty into a religious obligation. According to Muhammad ibn Abd al Wahhab's teachings, a Muslim must present a *bayah*, or oath of allegiance, to a Muslim ruler during his lifetime to ensure his redemption after death. The ruler, conversely, is owed unquestioned allegiance from his people as long as he leads the community according to the laws of God. The purpose of the Muslim community is to become the living embodiment of God's laws, and it's the responsibility of the legitimate ruler to ensure that people know God's laws and live in conformity to them.[3]

The Ulama (Religious Leaders) and the Saudi Government

How are religious leaders aligned with the Saudi Government and what impact does that alliance have on the system of governance? An understanding of the answer to this question provides insights into why it's difficult for the government to act unilaterally in such matters as, for instance, completely lifting the restriction on women driving.

The ulama, or Islamic religious leaders, served a unique role by providing religious legitimacy for Saudi rule. The Kingdom's ulama includes religious scholars, qadis (judges), lawyers, seminary teachers, and the prayer leaders (imams) of the mosques. Members of the Council of Senior Ulama, an official body created by Faisal in 1971, serve as a forum for regular consultation between the monarch and the religious establishment.

King Fahd continued the precedent set by Faisal and Khalid of meeting weekly with Council of Senior Ulama members who resided in Riyadh. The Council of Senior Ulama had a symbiotic relationship with the Saudi government. In return for official recognition of their special religious authority, the leading ulama provided tacit approval and, when requested, public sanction for potentially controversial policies. Because Saudi kings esteemed their Islamic credentials as custodians of the holy cities of Mecca and Medina, they considered ulama support critical.

Historically, the royal family maintained close ties with the ulama, especially with members of the Al ash Shaykh. The Al ash Shaykh included the several hundred direct male descendants of the eighteenth-

---

[3] Metz, Helen Chapin, ed. *Saudi Arabia: A Country Study*. Washington: GPO for the Library of Congress.

century religious reformer Abd al Wahhab. The Al Saud dynastic founder, Muhammad ibn Saud, had married a daughter of Abd al Wahhab, and subsequent intermarriage between the two families reinforced their political alliance. The mother of King Faisal, for example, was the daughter of an Al ash Shaykh qadi who was a direct descendant of Muhammad ibn Abd al Wahhab. The preeminence of the Al ash Shaykh thus derived not only from its reputation for religious erudition but also from its position as part of the country's ruling elite.[4]

Religious Police

Who are they and what role do they play in policing women?

Islamic religious police (mutaween) is the police force responsible for the enforcement of Sharia in some Muslim-majority countries. The Mutaween in Saudi Arabia are tasked with enforcing Sharia as defined by the government, specifically by the Committee for the Promotion of Virtue and the Prevention of Vice (CPVPV). The Mutaween of the CPVPV consists of more than 3,500 officers in addition to thousands of volunteers...often accompanied by a police escort. They have the power to arrest unrelated males and females caught socializing, ...[and] to enforce Islamic dress-codes (headscarves and black robes known as abayas), and store closures during the prayer time. They enforce Muslim dietary laws, prohibit the consumption or sale of alcoholic beverages and pork, and seize banned consumer products and media regarded as anti-Islamic (such as CDs/DVDs of various Western musical groups, television shows and film which has material contrary to Sharia law or Islam itself).[5]

Extent of Veil Covering

Why do women in Saudi Arabia cover their faces to varying degrees?

It is noted that some of the women in the book have chosen to show their faces and some have not. The information provided below sheds light on some of the considerations they may make in determining the extent to wish they choose to cover up.

Wahhabi emphasis on conformity makes of external appearance and behavior a visible expression of inward faith. Therefore, whether one conforms in dress, in prayer, or in a host of other activities becomes a public statement of whether one is a true Muslim. Because adherence to

---

[4] Ibid
[5] http://en.wikipedia.org/wiki/Islamic_religious_police (accessed March 2015)

the true faith is demonstrable in tangible ways, the Muslim community can visibly judge the quality of a person's faith by observing that person's actions. In this sense, public opinion becomes a regulator of individual behavior.

It is also underscored that chastity and sexual modesty are highly valued. Applied primarily to women, these values are tied to family honor and also to the belief of religious obligation. Specific Quranic verses enjoin modesty upon women and, to a lesser degree, upon men; and women are viewed as being responsible for sexual temptation (jitna). Although this attitude is ancient in the Middle East and found to some degree throughout the area in modern times, it has taken on religious significance in Islam through interpretations of Muslim theologians.

The veiling and separation of women were considered mechanisms to ensure sexual modesty. In practice, the effect of veiling and separation also ensured the continuing dependence of women on men. Some families adopted more liberal standards than others in defining the extent of veiling and separation, but the underlying value of sexual modesty was almost universal. Because the separation of women from unrelated men was accepted as a moral imperative, most activities of a woman outside her home required the mediation of a servant or a man. The continuing dependence of women on men, in effect, perpetuated the family as a patriarchal unit. Control of women ensured female chastity and thus family honor as well as the patrilineal character of the family. In Saudi society in general, the role of women was basic to maintaining the structure of the family and therefore of society.[6]

Male Guardianship

Do Saudi women have to have male guardians?

The simple answer is yes, though the official law, if not the custom, requiring a guardian's permission for a woman to seek employment was repealed in 2008.

Under Saudi law, all females must have a male guardian (Wali), typically a father, brother or husband (a mahram). Girls and women are forbidden from traveling, conducting official business, or undergoing certain medical procedures without permission from their male guardians. The guardian has duties to, and rights over, the woman in many aspects of civic life.

---

[6] Metz, Helen Chapin, ed. *Saudi Arabia: A Country Study*. Washington: GPO for the Library of Congress.

Legal guardianship of women by a male, is practiced in varying degrees and encompasses major aspects of women's lives. The system is said to emanate from social conventions, including the importance of protecting women, and from religious precepts on travel and marriage, although these requirements were arguably confined to particular situations. Depending on the guardian, women may need their guardian's permission for: marriage and divorce; travel, if under 45; education; employment; opening a bank account; elective surgery, particularly when sexual in nature.

In 2012 the Saudi Arabian government implemented a new policy to help with the enforcement on the traveling restrictions for women. Under this new policy, Saudi Arabian men receive a text message on their mobile phones whenever a woman under their custody leaves the country, even if she is traveling with her guardian.[7]

Social Stratification

What role does tribal affiliation play in arranged marriages and what's the basis for social stratification in Saudi Arabia? A related question is whether being educated elevates one's social class?

Tribal affiliation constitutes a major status category based on bloodline. At the top of the tribal status category were the qabila (families that claim purity of descent from one of two eponymous Arab ancestors, Adnan or Qahtan), and could therefore claim to possess asl, the honor that stemmed from nobility of origin. To some extent, tribal status could be correlated to occupation, yet manual labor in general, but particularly tanning hides and metal work, was considered demeaning for individuals of qabila status. Qabila families considered themselves distinct from and distinctly superior to khadira, nontribal families, who could not claim qabila descent.

Khadira include most tradesmen, artisans, merchants, and scholars, and constituted the bulk of the urban productive population of pre-oil Arabia. Marriage between individuals of qabila and khadira status was not normally considered. The claim to qabila status was maintained by patrilineal descent; therefore, qabila families were concerned to observe strict rules of endogamy (marriage back into the paternal line) so that status might be maintained and children, who were considered to belong to the family of the father, not the mother, would not suffer the taint of mixed blood. Within the qabila status group, however, there were status

---

[7] http://en.wikipedia.org/wiki/Women's_rights_in_Saudi_Arabia#Male_guardians (accessed March 2015)

differentials, some groups being considered inferior precisely because they had once intermarried with khadira and were unable to claim purity of descent.

In contemporary Saudi Arabia, new status categories based on education and economic advantage have begun to undermine the importance of tribal affiliation and is having an homogenizing effect on this barrier to social integration. An additional status category based on bloodline was that of ashraf, those who claimed descent from the Prophet Muhammad. The ashraf were significant in the Hijaz but far less so in Najd. These status categories based on blood have were in the 1990s being transcended by status groups based on religion, commerce, professions, and political power. Religious authority, for example, constituted an additional category of status.

To some extent, as secular education became more valued and greater economic rewards accrued to those with technical and administrative skills, the status of the ulama declined. Merchants constitute an additional elite status category based on wealth. Many of the traditional merchant class, especially merchants from the Hijaz and the Eastern Province, lost influence as Saudi rulers ceased borrowing from them and began to compete with them, using oil resources to create a new merchant class favoring Najdis. The rulers also used preferential recruitment for administrative personnel from Najdi tribes, who in turn used their position to favor other Najdis and Najdi businesses. The result has been the creation of powerful administrative and commercial classes supplanting older elite groups based outside Najd.

Marriage

What are some of the pros and cons of marriage for women in Saudi Arabia?

While this is largely a personal matter, some insights into the customs and tradition of marriage are provided below.

Historically, marriage was not a sacrament but a civil contract, which had to be signed by witnesses and an amount of money (mehr) had to be paid by the husband to the wife. The contract might also add other stipulations, such as assuring the wife the right of divorce if the husband should take a second wife. Divorce could usually only be instigated by the husband, and because by law children belonged to the father, who could take custody of them after a certain age (the age varied with the Islamic legal school, but was usually seven for boys and puberty for girls), legally a wife and mother could be detached from her children at the wish of her husband.

When women married, they might become incorporated into the household of the husband but not into his family. A woman did not take her husband's name but kept the name of her father because legally women were considered to belong to the family of their birth throughout their lives.

Many in Saudi Arabia interpreted the retention of a woman's maiden name, as well as her retention of control over personal property as allowed under Islamic law, as an indication of women's essential independence from a husband's control under the Islamic system. Legally, a woman's closest male relative, such as a father or brother, was obligated to support her if she were divorced or widowed.

Because the prerogatives of divorce, polygyny, and child custody lay with the husband, women in Saudi Arabia appeared to be at a considerable disadvantage in marriage. However, these disadvantages were partially offset by a number of factors. The first was that children were emotionaly attached to mothers, and when children, especially sons, were grown, their ties to the mother secured her a place of permanence in the husband's family. Second, marriages were most often contracted by agreement between families, uniting cousins, or individuals from families seeking to expand their circle of alliances and enhance their prestige, so that a successful marriage was in the interest of, and the desire of, both husband and wife. In addition, Islamic inheritance laws guaranteed a share of inheritance to daughters and wives, so that many women in Saudi Arabia personally held considerable wealth. Because women by law were entitled to full use of their own money and property, they had economic independence to cushion the impact of divorce, should it occur. Most important, custody of children was in practice a matter for family discussion, not an absolute regulated by religion. Furthermore, judges of the Sharia courts, according to informal observations, responded with sympathy and reason when women attempted to initiate divorce proceedings or request the support of the court in family-related disputes.[8]

---

[8] Metz, Helen Chapin, ed. *Saudi Arabia: A Country Study.* Washington: GPO for the Library of Congress.

The Fight to Educate Women

Why has there been a battle to educate women?

"Women and Education in Saudi Arabia: Challenges and Achievements" (A. Hamdan, 2005)[9] provides key insights into the answer to this question.

...King Faisal convinced tribal bedouins of the importance of formal schooling for women [in the late 1950s]. His wife, Iffat Al Thunayan, had pushed for it and in 1956 she established the first school for girls.

The prospect of Saudi girls travelling through the public streets every day to attend school aroused alarm in the extremely conservative Saudi society. Yet, Faisal and Iffat were so committed to educating girls and planned for the first women's academy located in Jeddah. The academy was named, *Dar Al Hanan*, "The House of the Affection."

In 1957, the local press got a green light from officials and King Faisal to explain the objectives of *Dar Al Hanan*. [It was explained that] one of the main aims of the school was to raise good mothers based on Islamic essence and modern educational theories. Iffat argued with many conservative religious scholars saying that the place where a child learns religion and manners is in the home, therefore the spirituality of future generations would be improved through mothers who had received schooling and education. In 1960, a national committee consisting of members of the conservative religious scholars insisted on controlling and supervising the education of girls throughout the country.

Though King Faisal supported women's right to achieve their goals, he was not able to convince his public at the beginning. He had to send an official force to Buraydah in 1963 to keep the girls' school open when public rioting threaten to close it down.

Though he ruled that girls' schooling be mandatory and obligatory, a ruling that continues to the present time, he did not force parents to educate girls. He endeavored to figure out how to [combine] tradition and development. He rejected the idea that in order to modernize Saudi Arabia its past would have to be erased, and he believed that slow and steady change was better than violent, disruptive attempts to force change.

He saw a need to enlighten his people's understanding of Islamic teachings regarding women's education and whenever faced resistance he would

---

[9] Amani Hamdan, "Women and Education in Saudi," International Education Journal, 2005, 6(1), 42-64.

ask, "Is there anything in the Holy Quran which forbids the education of women?" He further stated, "We have no cause for argument, God enjoins learning on every Muslim man and women."

The conservative religious scholars approved the education of girls only with certain conditions and constraints. Girls' schools are surrounded by high walls and backup screens behind the entry area doors. Each girls' school, college or university is assigned at least two men who are usually in their 50s or 60s who are responsible to check the identity of those who enter the school, deliver and pick up the mail and generally to safeguard the girls inside the school until they are picked up by their fathers or brothers. To date, physical education and fitness facilities are not available for women. School buses for women have not escaped the rigid rules. Since women are not allowed to drive, the buses are driven by elderly men. Girls enter the bus from the back door and are usually supervised by a female relative of the driver.

By 1981, the number of girls enrolled in schools was almost equal to the number of boys. The administration of girls' education was controlled by the Directorate General of Girls' Education, an organization staffed by conservative religious scholars. The purpose of educating a girl, as stated by the Directorate General, was 'to bring her up in a proper Islamic way so as to perform her duty in life, be an ideal and successful housewife and a good mother, ready to do things which suit her nature as teaching, nursing, and medical treatment.'

Segregation in the Higher Education System

Why are the sexes separated throughout the education system?

The Quran warns that the intermingling of the sexes can lead to "seduction and the evil consequences that might follow." Wahhabism, in its strict orthodoxy, interprets the Quran's cautioning by tightly restricting any type of interaction among unmarried and unrelated men and women. Accordingly, the Saudi education system limits women's access to labor markets and participation in the global economy. This remains the case in spite of the consistently higher achievement of women over men in secondary and higher education, in spite of women university graduates flooding into the job market by the tens of thousands, and in spite of an economy vastly overburdened with foreign workers whose positions could be filled by Saudi women. Women have been excluded from studying various disciplines such as engineering but have been permitted to study others such as dentistry, education, medicine, nursing, and public administration that have been seen to be an extension of women's domestic roles and consistent with stereotypical women's qualities of caring and nurturing.

Status of Female University Graduates

To what extent are women making strides in higher education?

When the Kingdom was established in 1932, education was available to very few people, and it wasn't until 1964 that the first government school for girls was built. Today, female students make up over half of the more than 6 million students currently enrolled in Saudi schools and universities. According to information provided by the Saudi Embassy, "today, Saudi Arabia's education system includes 25 public and 27 private universities, with more planned; some 30,000 schools; and a large number of colleges and other institutions."[10]

At present, it's estimated by the World Bank that at least 60 percent of university students in Saudi Arabia are Saudi females. Insights about the status of education for women are presented in *Women's Education in Saudi Arabia: The Way Forward*,[11] as follows:

Education in Saudi Arabia is an area in which women have experienced significant progress. The Saudi government has gone to considerable effort to increase girls' access to education and reduce the gender gap at different educational levels. Women's education has brought about a number of social developments in the country, such as a reduction in fertility and mortality rates, an improvement in health and nutrition, and an increase in female participation in the labor force. However, lingering social norms, local traditions, and the structure of the system of public education have been constraints on women's realization of their equal opportunities in society and their full participation in the labor market. Today, reforming the educational system for girls has become a priority as well as a great challenge for the Saudi government.

Saudi Arabia has invested large amounts of money in the system of public education.

However, the substantial increase has not resulted in an equal increase in women's production output. Investing in women's education has led to a quantitative expansion of the number of girls' schools, to the detriment of the quality provided and the skills developed. Educational reform in the country has focused for the past few years mainly on infrastructure changes, building schools, hiring a large number of teachers, and issuing a loaded curriculum.

---

[10] http://www.saudiembassy.net/about/country-information/education/ (Accessed May 2015)
[11] Booz & Co., Women's Education in Saudi Arabia: The Way Forward, http://www.ideationcenter.com/media/file/Womens_Education_in_SaudiArabia_Advance_Look_FINALv9.pdf, (Accessed April 2015)

A discrepancy exists between the type of skills provided for in the curricula of public education for girls and those needed in the labor market. The absence of those skills has led to a high unemployment rate among Saudi women and a high participation rate for foreign labor in the country. Educational reforms should focus on improving the equity outcomes of the system of public education for girls for further training and lifelong learning, while promoting employability, productivity, and social inclusion.

A more flexible perception of women's participation in the workforce is needed. This would generate more job opportunities for Saudi women, contributing to national income, while reducing the country's dependence on foreign labor. Further educational reforms and developments, improving the quality of girls' education and emphasizing their role in community development, should strive to produce a society committed to mobilizing its human resources for a competitive market.

The Shura Council

Professor Dr. Selwa Al-Hazzaa, Member Shura Council

What is the significance for women of the Shura Council?

The appointment of 30 women to the Council by the late King Abdullah was one of the single greatest leaps forward in Saudi history for women's empowerment, along with the King's declaration that women could vote and run in the 2015 elections. The appointment of women to the Council presents an unprecedented opportunity to raise the voices of women and to have those voices heard.

One of the women featured in this book, Dr. Selwa Al-Hazzaa, is one of the 30 women appointed to the Council.

> The Consultative Assembly of Saudi Arabia also known as *Majlis as-Shura* or *Shura Council* is the formal advisory body of Saudi Arabia. It has limited powers in government; it has the power to propose laws to the King and cabinet but it cannot pass or enforce laws, which is a power reserved for the King. It has 150 members, all of whom are appointed by the King. The Assembly does, however, have the power to interpret laws, as well as examine annual reports referred to it by state ministries and agencies. It can also advise the King on policies he submits to it, along with international treaties and economic plans. The Assembly is also authorized to review the country's annual budget, and call in ministers for questioning.
>
> The influence of the Assembly in its present form comes from its responsibility for the Kingdom's five-year development plans, from which the annual budgets are derived, its ability to summon government officials for questioning, and its role as policy debate forum.
>
> In January 2013, King Abdullah issued two royal decrees, granting women thirty seats on the council, and stating that women must always hold at least a fifth of the seats on the council. According to the decrees, the female council members must be 'committed to Islamic Shariah disciplines without any violations' and be 'restrained by the religious veil.'
>
> The decrees also said that the female council members would be entering the council building from special gates, sit in seats reserved for women and pray in special worshipping places.[12]

Segregation in the Work Place

The Saudi government recently ordered that shops that employ both men and women set up separation walls to ensure that the two sexes are separated while they work. Stores must erect barriers not shorter than 1.6 meters to separate male and female employees. Retailers were given 30 days to install the walls, or risk sanctions. The legislation was issued by Labour Minister Adel Faqih, with the help of Abdullatif al-Sheikh, the head of the Commission for the Promotion of Virtue and Prevention of Vice, commonly known as the religious police, according to local press. Essentially, women in Saudi Arabia can work either in all-women factories or in lingerie and cosmetics shops. The latter has been allowed since June 2011, when the Saudi leadership issued an order for lingerie and cosmetics shops to replace their male staffers, most of whom were Asian, with Saudi women.

---

[12] http://en.wikipedia.org/wiki/Consultative_Assembly_of_Saudi_Arabia (accessed March 2015)

As a result of the legislation, authorities announced that 44,000 jobs were created for Saudi women, for whom the unemployment rate currently stands at 36 percent, according to the Central Department of Statistics and Information. Saudi women account for only 7 percent of citizens employed by private companies.[13]

Driving

Why are women banned from driving?

First, it must be underscored that many conservative Saudi women do not support loosening traditional gender roles and restrictions because to them, "Saudi Arabia is the closest thing to an ideal and pure Islamic nation." Those in this camp also eschew imported western values.

It's also noted that because the infrastructure, both social and physical, for driving women around is so well established and entrenched the inability for women to drive themselves does not impose the same level of inconvenience it would in western nations. In addition, women do not customarily act alone or outside the family so the requirement and reasons to drive –and the places to drive to–are limited.

But, it's not about the driving *per se* for less conservative women; it's about its symbolism. Not having the right to drive is symbolic of being treated as a child and as a person without agency.

Just as the ban on women driving is symbolic for the banned women, it's also symbolic for the religious clerics—but for different reasons; to them, giving women freedom of movement makes them more vulnerable to sin.

Participation in Sport

What is the rationale for restricting women from participating in sports?

Sarah Attar and Wojdan Shaherkani were the first Saudi women to take part in any Olympics when they represented their country in London in 2012. If they had not been allowed to take part, Saudi Arabia would have been the only one of the 204 competing countries not to have any female representatives. Their participation attracted a range of opinions concerned about whether this represented an important advance for women's rights in Saudi Arabia. Participation in any sport is very difficult for any Saudi woman, as the Ministry of Education bans physical education for girls. The rationale behind the ban ranges from claims that sport will lead to corrupt morals and lesbianism, to sport being masculine and damaging for female health and psyche. In 2013, Saudi women were first allowed to ride bicycles, although only around parks

---

[13] http://rt.com/news/saudi-women-walls-sexes-968/

and other "recreational areas." They must also be dressed in full body coverings and be accompanied by a male relative. In 2013, the Saudi government sanctioned sports for girls in private schools for the first time.[14]

—◆—

I n conclusion, the stories of the women in the book have shown what is possible for Saudi women to achieve when they are given a chance. They are capable of making major contributions in many professional disciplines that benefit Saudi society and the world, while also holding fast to their religious beliefs and cultural norms. In the future, at this rate of positive demonstration, it is expected that Saudi women will increasingly become examples and role models of success for women to emulate all over the world.

As the numbers of Saudi female graduates continue to swell, we are reminded that is a mathematical fact that it is impossible to add by subtracting. Thus, for Saudi Arabia to continue to develop, thrive, and realize its goals of Saudization the contributions of women must increasingly be *added in*. The examples of the women featured in the book are proof positive that such contributions can be substantial.

—◆—

[14] Ibid.

About
Professor, Dr. Selwa Al-Hazzaa MD, FRCS (OPHTH)

Dr. Al-Hazzaa was born in Riyadh and is married to Mr. Abdulla Al-Obaidalla, Executive Director of University Certificates Equivalency, Ministry of Higher Education; they have three children: Meshaal– 9/90 (Medical Student Graduate); Naif – 8/91 (Business Graduate); and Hala – 9/92 (Engineer Graduate).

Dr. Al-Hazzaa is a Consultant of Ophthalmology at the King Faisal Specialist Hospital & Research Center (KFSH & RC) in Riyadh (since 1993), and Head of Ophthalmology since 1997 (first Saudi female doctor to hold this position); she has also served as the Acting Chairman of Ophthalmology since 2012, and as the Chairman of Ophthalmology since March 2015. While Dr. Al-Hazzaa's accomplishments are too many to enumerate, some highlights of her illustrious career include:

- Being appointed by King Abdullah on January 11, 2013, among 30 women, as a member to the Majlis Alshura (Saudi Parliament);
- Being the first female doctor Professor, College of Medicine, Al-Faisal University (2011) and Senior Advisor to Minister of Health, Riyadh, Saudi Arabia;
- Being the first female doctor member of the Executive Board of the Saudi Ophthalmologic Society (SOS) in 1996 and the first Saudi female doctor appointed to the Medical Advisory Council of the King Faisal Specialist Hospital & Research Center, Riyadh, Saudi Arabia (1995);
- Being a member of the Editorial Board of the *Saudi Journal of Ophthalmology* in 1997; Associate Editor in 1998-2008 (first female doctor); and member of the Editorial Board of the *Ophthalmic Genetics Journal* in the USA in 1997-2005;
- Being the first female doctor to serve as the Assistant Editor of the *Middle East Journal of Ophthalmology* from 1992-1996; being on the Editorial Board of the *Archives of Ophthalmology*, since 2005, and the *Chinese Journal* of *Ophthalmology*, since 2006, representing the Middle East.

Dr. Al-Hazzaa is also a Senior Clinical Scientist and Consultant in Genetics at the King Faisal Specialist Hospital & Research Center. Owing to her many accomplishments, she was named "Arab Woman of the Year" in the field of Medicine & Community Services in 2005 & 2006 by the Arab Women Studies Center in Paris, France and chosen by *Forbes International* Magazine chose as one of "The Most Powerful Arab Women for year 2005." Despite holding numerous positions, Dr. Al-Hazzaa has also made many medical breakthroughs, which include, for instance, introducing the Protocol for "Retinopathy of Prematurity;" being the first in the Middle East to treat "Retinopathy of Prematurity" using the diode laser. She was also was the first to use Photodynamic Therapy to treat "Age Related Macular Degeneration" (ARMD) in the Gulf Region and the first Physician to use Avastin (Bevizumib) for patients in Middle East.

In addition to the foregoing, Dr. Al-Hazzaa has published 66 international papers, including seven book chapters and is currently undertaking 12 research projects. Much in demand, Dr. Al-Hazzaa has also given 388 international and national television, radio, and newspaper interviews, not including sparing her valuable time herein to share her remarkable story. ❧

Professor Selwa A.F. Al-Hazzaa, MD, FRCS

Member, Saudi Shura Council
and
Chairman of Ophthalmology Department, King Faisal Specialist Hospital & Research Center

"One Grain of Sand"

Early Life

There's poetry to sand. It's a metaphor for the passage of time and for forcing the realization that while it's uncountable in its aggregation, one tiny grain can temporarily blind the strongest person and just a few more can bring to a screeching halt the most highly sophisticated jet engine.

Dr. Al-Hazzaa giving a speech in the Shura Council

My story exists within this metaphor. On the one hand, I am part of the uncountable aggregation and fully embrace my culture and rest easily within the sands of our time and traditions; while on the other, my accomplishments demonstrate that transformation and tradition can coexist.

My story is contrasted with that of my mother, my first role model. There are only fourteen years difference in our ages but because she was born before schooling began for females in 1960, she was forced to be illiterate. I understand that this was our tradition at the time. My mother also accepted her place within the traditions of her time but that didn't stop her from advocating for her daughters to be educated.

Dr. Al-Hazzaa, Medical Doctor

My father also adhered to the traditions of his time but understood, metaphorically speaking, that one could hold more sand by loosely cupping one's hands and lifting rather than by attempting to grip it. Thus, when his only brother, who was 20 years older than he and who controlled the family's wealth and power, told my father that he was not allowed to learn to read and write "as there was no need for it because we had everything," my father pretended to be blind, and used a cane so that he could have an excuse to study in the mosque with blind students at night.

Each night while his brother and mother were sleeping my father would secretly learn to read and write. Imagine 12 years later what a shock it was for his brother when my father told him that he had received a scholarship to attend a university in America.

How could this happen, my uncle wondered? After all, he thought that my father was illiterate like himself and his ancestors before him.

My uncle wasn't the only one that opposed broad education; my mother's maternal uncles went even further and actually obstructed the late King Faisal's efforts to open schools in Buraida at the time. The opposition didn't stop there. In fact, so serious was my maternal grandfather's opposition, not only to education in general but specifically to the notion of going abroad to become educated, that he threatened to disown my mother if she went to America, the "Land of the Infidels", with my father.

At the end of the day, despite opposition from every corner, the one my father really had to convince was his older brother. Finally, after numerous attempts to persuade

Dr. Al-Hazzaa during Opening Ceremony of Saudi-US Business Forum

his brother to let him travel to America to pursue his education, my uncle agreed on the condition that he leave his five daughters behind in Saudi Arabia to be properly raised while he studied. My father, however, refused to accept these terms, or to leave his wife behind.

My mother, despite all of the opposition she faced, went off to America at 19 years old with my father and five young girls in tow, to Tucson, Arizona, where I was raised from the time I was six years old.

Perhaps my desire to be like that proverbial "single grain of sand that makes all the difference" had its foundation in my intuitive understanding of and appreciation for our unique societal context. From the very beginning I knew that I wanted to be somebody in the world and my parents did not discourage me from thinking this way. To the contrary, my parents understood me and knew that I could not and would not be held down. When my father defied tradition and the will of his and his wife's family to pursue his own education and education for his family, I realized the value that was being placed on education and concluded that becoming educated was the way to become somebody in the world.

"The Juice Has to be Worth the Squeeze"

The thing about societal change is that, if you are lucky, it happens in small smart steps. I'm personally in favor of evolution; not revolution. On a personal, family, professional, and societal basis the question I must always ask myself as I navigate my world and the world around me is: "What are the small smart steps I can take?"

To understand my journey, you have to understand where I come from. I am originally from Buraida in Al-Qassim region, which is reputedly the most conservative and religious part of Saudi Arabia. When we speak of being conservative, we also have to understand what is being conserved. Such conservation embodies a complex web of traditions, beliefs, customs, religious understanding, and other factors that combine to constitute our culture.

Historically, Al-Qassim region is known as the "alimental basket" of the country. Our family's wealth derives from real estate, and as in most countries, those closest to the land tend to hold on tightest to the old traditions.

Our conservative culture in the heartland of the country has not historically embraced higher education for women nor has it held education in high esteem as the path to enlightenment, societal acceptance, wealth or happiness. In fact, when I was born in 1962 over 60 percent of the population was still nomadic. To break out of the mold, and to take the kind of unprecedented steps my father took to broaden his education, was no small feat.

How far one is willing to go to hold onto the desirable aspects of the past, while simultaneously leapfrogging into the future, is a question that has to be asked and answered as situations arise.

As Saudis, such questions are invariably asked in the context of weighing the impact of personal decisions on the entire family at large. It's important to underscore that social relations in Saudi Arabia are indirectly tied to family considerations and that the family is the fundamental and essential repository of every individual's personal identity. Although there are some variations in the family structure, the basic pattern is the same and the differences are largely of degree. Simply put, the Saudi family is of an extended type.

Education Creates Longer Lasting Impressions than Footprints in the Sand

Just as sand is the essential component of concrete; education is the essential foundation for sustainable development, in my view. My father deeply understood this as well, which is why when a young man was unexpectedly brought forth by his family to my family and asked for my hand in marriage, my father agreed. My father's condition was to "allow" me to continue my studies and to work subsequently.

1st female to cut a ribbon at an all-male ceremony

I know why my father agreed to the choice of my future husband. It was because my "intended" was from Unaizah, the 2nd largest city in the Al Qassim Region, which is known as the Paris of Najd and also for having outspoken women who wield substantial influence. This was important because my father reckoned that having such a background would increase my chances of having a lasting marriage, given that I was extremely independent and strong willed.

For my part, in what was seen as a radical departure from the norm at the time 26 years ago, I actually insisted on having my intended visit with me in my home, of course under supervised conditions, so that we could get to know each other. By our sixth meeting over a six month period, I knew he was the one for me. He highly respected my independence and wanted a partner in life and not just a

Dr. Al-Hazzaa interviewing the 1st pilot of the late King Abdullah

marriage. Furthermore, he was just as much in the dark as I was about the marriage arrangements his family made for us.

We learned that our common bond was our mutual respect for education and we agreed that we both must obtain it and then use it wisely and productively.

The Road Less Travelled

Essentially, I was a person straddled between two worlds. I was raised in the U.S. with English as my mother tongue yet my roots were grounded in the most conservative region in Saudi Arabia. Over the years, I tempered my acceptance of some of our traditions, like that of arranged marriages, but gradually began to speak up and to impose some conditions of my own. For

Dr. Al-Hazzaa in her office

instance, in the case of my arranged marriage my conditions included: agreeing with the choice of my mate; getting to know the person before marrying; and insisting that the selected person agree to my independent character, my continual quest for knowledge and to my insistence on applying my knowledge professionally.

While education has been the central theme of my life and is the reason why I am where I am today, the opportunities I have had to acquire higher education were unprecedented at the time. This is not surprising given that according to UNESCO estimates, in the 1950s more than 90 percent of the Saudi Arabian population was illiterate, yet only three decades later I was pursuing education at the highest levels.

Basic education, as opposed to higher education, garnered more support starting from the late eighteenth century when the Wahhabi movement encouraged the spread of Islamic education for all Muslim believers. Because the purpose of Islamic education was to ensure that believers would understand God's laws and live his or her life in accordance with them, classes for reading and memorizing the Holy Quran along with selections from the hadith were sponsored in towns and villages throughout the peninsula. At the most basic level, education took place in the kuttab, a class of Quran recitation for children usually attached to a mosque, or as a private tutorial held in the home under the direction of a male or female professional Quran reader, which was usually the case for girls. Students who wished to pursue their studies beyond the elementary level could attend an informal network of scholarly lectures (halaqat) offering instruction in Islamic jurisprudence, Arabic language, Quranic commentaries (tafsir), hadith, literature, rhetoric, and sometimes arithmetic and history.

For women, the goal of education has been ideologically tied to religion. It has been stated in education planning documents that "the purpose of educating a girl is to bring her up in a proper Islamic way so as to enable her to perform her duty in life, be an ideal and successful housewife and a good mother, who is ready to do things that suit her nature such as teaching, nursing and medical treatment." Education policy specifically recognized "the right of women to obtain suitable education on equal footing with men in light of Islamic laws."

In practice, the inequalities of opportunity in education have stemmed from the religious and social imperative of gender segregation. Gender segregation has historically been required at all levels of public education and demanded in public areas and businesses by religiously conservative groups as well as by social convention. Because the social perception was that men would put the knowledge and skills acquired to productive use, fewer resources were dedicated to women's higher education than to men's.

Such viewpoints failed to foresee the emergence of women like me, however, whose aspirations and capabilities would incline and enable them to not only be productive, but to break new ground in doing so.

It wasn't easy breaking through and my options for what I was allowed to study were limited. First, as a woman, it was considered going out on a limb to seek the level education I sought. Secondly, I had only two options of what to pursue: to be a teacher or a doctor. I didn't want to be either of those things but my dad persuaded me to pursue medicine. He had three compelling reasons. First, he argued, that as a medical doctor, I would be respected and no one could dismiss my body of knowledge. Secondly, he suggested that the field of medicine was considered noble. Finally, he argued that the demand for doctors in Saudi Arabia far outstripped the supply and therefore my services would be needed.

As for myself, I came to realize that through medicine I could become "somebody." I always wanted to be somebody and realize my dream of representing my country one day. But I didn't just want to be a regular doctor, I wanted to become a specialist and thus had to overcome yet another obstacle because the fields of specialization open to females were limited.

Seeing the Light

Ophthalmology was one of the only specializations open to me as a woman in Saudi Arabia; so it chose me rather than the other way around. I did my part; I qualified against all odds and secured one of the limited entry slots. After finally completing my medical degree in Saudi Arabia I wanted to do a residency abroad. Again, it wasn't easy to go down this road.

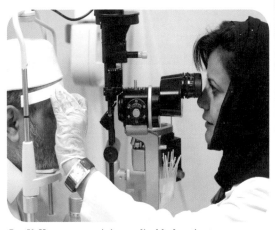
Dr. Al-Hazzaa examining a disabled patient

The ulama (religious elders) frowned on women going overseas to study and so did our families but I didn't want to lose this once in a lifetime opportunity. The Saudi conferred residency in Ophthalmology was the first and only residency in Saudi Arabia, and as it was recognized in the U.S. I could continue my fellowship there.

While studying Ophthalmology wasn't my initial choice, it dawned on me that this choice was the right one for me as it paved the way for me to be the trailblazer I always wanted to be. I became the first Saudi women qualified abroad in Ophthalmology.

There was another positive social aspect related to my field, I realized. The practice of it requires that certain gender work place segregation norms be relaxed, and that's a good thing. After all, gender separation throughout the course of study in Saudi Arabia comes at a cost. It's not just the matter of differing quality of education; it's also a missed opportunity to get to know each other during our early years of study. I will never forget that one day during my fellowship in the U.S. at Johns Hopkins University my husband brought a Saudi colleague home for coffee. I recognized the man as the person who had been reluctant to sit next to females during our residency program

Dr. Al-Hazzaa on Capitol Hill in the U.S. with Senator McCain

together in Saudi Arabia. I asked him frankly: "Why did you shun me; why were you reluctant to sit next to me?" He told me honestly that he had never had any exposure to Saudi females and did not know how to react.

Light is Good from Whichever Lamp it Shines

Being a trailblazer is rewarding and exhilarating, but it's not easy.

I remember that in 1986, as a first year resident, I won the award for the best research paper, in competition against the male staffers and residents who were studying as well. The ceremony was held in Jeddah so I decided to comply with prevailing customs and took my brother as "my guardian," even though he was 12 years younger than me. I was so excited about getting the award and waited anxiously in my seat during the opening ceremony for the announcement to come but it never came. I couldn't believe it. I went up to the announcer during intermission and asked him what happened. He said, "Doctor, we never expected the name of the recipient to be a female. When we realized that it was a female and that there would be television cameras streaming the event, with high official dignitaries in the audience, we decided to have your recognition during the educational conference in the days to follow so that your recognition (as a woman) would not be broadcasted to the public."

It was a stark reality to face. There had been at least 200 people in attendance; most importantly, my younger brother was there and I wanted and needed him to report back the news of my award acceptance to my parents. Because pursuing higher education as a female at the time was not exactly applauded nor welcomed by most members of my extended family, it was particularly important to excel. I persuasively negotiated with those in charge of the ceremony proceedings to—by whatever means necessary—announce my name during the ceremony opening on the main night. We struck the agreement that they would make the announcement after the intermission with the cameras turned off and I agreed to this compromise.

There are many times in my life and career where the reality of my situation as a female professional in Saudi Arabia has collided like a brick with cultural norms. Perhaps if I didn't't have my feet so firmly planted in two worlds, both in the West and in the Middle East, I wouldn't be as shocked.

Yet another jolting experience comes to mind. In 2002, I was asked to be an advisor to the Shura Council, though I had not fully appreciated that I was essentially being asked to be an advisor "behind the scenes." When the word leaked out that I was asked to serve in this role, as one of the first woman to do so, and the Council was confronted about it, Council officials flatly denied that I was playing this role. All at once I experienced one of the greatest recognitions that my society can confer, to be asked to be an advisor to the Shura Council, and yet one of the greatest humiliations to have my role disavowed.

It was true poetic justice when in a landmark move under the late King Abdullah in 2013, I was formally appointed as a member to the Shura Council a decade later.

Many Small Steps Add Up to a Giant Stride

Reflecting back on my negotiations with my betrothed, now my husband of 26 years, what was important to seal our deal was a shared common interest in wanting to make a difference in society. So far, some of my small steps have enabled me to accomplish this goal, but of course, my work isn't finished.

As a mother of three children, as a wife, as the Chairman of the Ophthalmology Department and practicing physician, as an academician teaching future medical physicians, and as a scientist and politician, I know that I am needed and that there's much for me to do. Among the many hats I wear, I now have one of the heaviest on my head. My new frontier is to contribute my wisdom to the governing body of our society, the Shura Council, in order to make a positive impact and to be a force for social change.

Dr. Al-Hazzaa with two of her children

Dr. Al-Hazzaa during a convocation ceremony at a university

In the lead up to being named as one of the first female members of the Shura Council, I recall that two years earlier I was working in my clinic seeing patients when my assistant interrupted me to tell me that I had an important call from Saudi TV; they had called numerous times and finally I had to take the call. To my shock I was asked to go on television immediately to give my opinion about the prospect of women being appointed to the Shura Council. Though I was in no way prepared to go on live television to discuss this matter, as I had no forewarning and wasn't wearing the appropriate attire (I wear my lab coat in the office), I nevertheless went on television and finally spilled out a secret.

I said publicly that I had already been an advisor to the Shura Council years before, though it was in secret, and I played a key role in the Shura Council becoming a part of the international Parliment.

First Do No Harm

First and foremost, I am a doctor. I have taken an oath to help people directly and this to me takes priority over my desire to help people indirectly. After all, it was through my discipline of medicine that I had proven myself, that I had become liberated, and had made major breakthroughs in science. So, when the call came in the year 2013 to

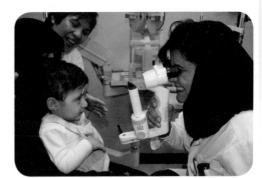
Dr. Al-Hazzaa examining a child

be appointed to the Shura Council, I had my own terms and conditions. I could not do it if it took me away from my clinical job. I go to the clinic every day and help people and I wanted to continue doing this. I also wanted to continue to undertake research, especially as I am the first and only Retina Geneticist in the Kingdom.

While it is a groundbreaking opportunity to be among the first women to serve on the Shura Council in the history of the Kingdom, I also had to continue in my administrative role running the department, as in the previous fifteen years, in the largest hospital in the Middle East. At that point I was asked to serve on the Council, I was already fully engaged and in charge of my life and a very full clinical schedule.

When the official announcement came on television on the weekend, I was in the kitchen cooking and had a goal I wanted to achieve at that moment, which was simply to make a delicious traditional lunch. After I accomplished that goal, I was happy to accept the many congratulatory calls.

I guess I was chosen because as everybody knows, "If you want something done, ask a busy person."

As I face this new challenge, here is what I know for sure: I love Saudi Arabia; it's my roots and my identity. I know that many things must change and that I will strive to be a positive force for change. I will fight for women's rights, for the rights of senior citizens and for those of the disabled; and importantly, I will fight against corruption at all costs.

I underscore that our fight to change what needs to be changed within our society is ours to undertake and no one else's. To the point: no one from the outside should interfere in our internal affairs because we know what to do and when to do it at an appropriate pace. We understand that it will take a little more time for some of the more conservative factions in our society—many of which are from my own hometown—but they are us and we are them. If we totally cut them off, we cut part of ourselves off. No, the way to go is gradually, in small smart steps. I am all for an evolution, but not a revolution.

THE ARAB WOMAN AWARDS 2015

Professor Dr. Selwa Al-Hazzaa, Head of Ophthalmology Department at King Faisal Specialist Hospital and member of the Shoura Council, received two awards for her Medical and Lifetime Achievements.

The Arab Woman Awards mission is to provide a culturally accepted platform to raise public awareness of the significant achievements of Arab women across the GCC & provide positive role models for young women. The ten-year vision is to have awarded over 500 inspirational, talented & deserving Arab women. The first awards were held in Dubai & now run annually in the United Arab Emirates, Qatar, Kuwait, and the Kingdom of Saudi Arabia.

About
Norah Abdallah Al-Faiz

Norah bint Abdallah Al-Faiz, (born 1956) is the first woman to hold a cabinet-level office in Saudi Arabia.

Early life and education

Norah Al-Faiz was born in Shaqraa in 1956. Al-Faiz received a Bachelor of Arts degree in Sociology from King Saud University in Riyadh in 1979. She also received a master's degree in Instructional Technologies from Utah State University in 1982.

Career

Upon returning to Saudi Arabia, Al-Faiz worked as a teacher. She became head principal of the girls' section at Prince Alwaleed bin Talal's Kingdom Schools.

Later, Al-Faiz served as the head of ministry of education's educational technology center, and a lecturer and head of the training board of the ministry's administration institute from 1983 to 1988. In 1993, she became ministry's educational supervisor for girls' private education. She was also appointed the director general of women's section of the institute of public administration in 1993, which she held until 2009. In addition, she worked as an associate professor in the department of education techniques from 1989 to 1995 at the College of Education, King Saud University.

Al-Faiz was named deputy minister of education in charge of women's affairs in February 2009 and is the first woman to direct girls' education in Saudi Arabia. She told that her appointment is "a source of pride for all women."

Al-Faiz currently serves as Advisor to the Ministry of Education. ❧

Norah Abdullah Al-Faiz

Former Vice Minister for Girls Education

Ministry of Education

"Education as a Whole"

"Open the door for her Excellency." This is what a government official said to my son as we were leaving the official's office. That was the first time I had ever been referred to as "Her Excellency." It was only one hour after having been appointed to the position of Vice Minister for Girls Education in the Ministry of Education in 2009. When I was referred to in this way, I knew what it meant: It would be a great a responsibility!

Being the first female to be appointed to the position of Vice Minister in the history of Saudi Arabia was at once a great honor and a great challenge. Any concerns in my mind about the challenges, however, were far outweighed by the unprecedented opportunity to serve in a position that would enable me to ensure and enhance educational opportunities for females and be a role model for other women.

The whole world took note of Norah's appointment. The following article was published in 2009 when Norah was appointed.

Norah Al-Faiz

By Liz Cheney Thursday, Apr. 30, 2009

Illustration for TIME by Jeffrey Smith

In Saudi Arabia small changes carry deep meaning, so the appointment earlier this year of Norah al-Faiz as Deputy Minister for Women's Education was nothing short of an earthquake. Educated at King Saud University and Utah State, al-Faiz is the first woman minister in Saudi history. The appointment of al-Faiz, in her early 50s, was the most significant sign yet of the quiet revolution under way since King Abdullah ascended the throne in 2005. The King also replaced his Minister of Justice, head of the religious police and Minister of Education with more moderate, reform-minded leaders.

Saudi reformers welcomed the changes, especially the appointment of al-Faiz, but the real test will be whether she is allowed the authority to get things done. The education of girls has long been a battleground within the kingdom. Al-Faiz faces practical difficulties too. She can't, for example, work face to face with male counterparts without violating the kingdom's strict religious code — so she has said she will conduct meetings through closed-circuit television. Her presence at the ministry has had an immediate impact on Saudi women, who had been unable to enter the building. No longer. "Now I am the deputy minister, and my door is open and accessible," alFaiz said after her appointment...

To appreciate the meaning of my appointment, it is important to understand the history of educating girls in Saudi Arabia.

Formal public schooling for girls in Saudi Arabia only dates to the 1960s, when the first official primary school for girls opened in Riyadh. Prior to this, informal schooling for both boys and girls primarily focused on teaching religious practices.

Initially, opening schools for girls was met with strong opposition in some parts of the Kingdom, where nonreligious education was viewed as irrelevant for serving the country's needs. Not surprisingly, back in the early 1960s, 22 percent of boys and only 2 percent of girls were enrolled in primary school. Fortunately, however, within a few years, public perception of the value of educating girls changed profoundly and soon the general population strongly favored it.

I was born in 1956, four years before the advent of formal public schooling for girls, in the Shaqraa Province 190 kilometers from Riyadh. I was part of the first generation of females that had the opportunity to be formally educated and attend public elementary school. This helped to set the stage in my young life, and, with my father's encouragement, I began to ponder the question that children all over the world raise when they are in the formal education process: "What shall I be when I grow up?"

In pondering the question of what "could I be" when I grew up, it's noteworthy that at the time of my pondering, women's education in Saudi Arabia was focused on preparing women to be good wives and mothers, and preparing them for jobs that were considered "acceptable" at the time, such as teaching and medical services that were "deemed to be suitable professions for women given their nature."

Though opportunities for women to become formally educated have grown over time that does not mean that the patriarchal nature of our society has changed. Women have always been and remain subordinate to men in every field. The empowerment of the girl child starts at home, first. When a father gives permission and encouragement to his daughters to dare to dream big, it's a big thing and a necessary precursor. Fortunately for me, my father, an Arabic teacher, was both educated and enlightened and encouraged me to have aspirations and to pursue them.

As the eldest of six brothers and three sisters I had a special place in our family. Perhaps owing to this and to the maturity it brings, my father saw something special in me and gave me permission to dream. My dreams were built – and expanded – on the foundation of education. In fact, my first dream was simply to be educated for its own sake without fully knowing how to apply my education. I was happy to attend King Saud University, where I obtained an undergraduate degree in sociology in 1978. Meanwhile, I followed the traditional path at that time by marrying before I graduated.

After graduation, I was employed as a high school sociology teacher, which is a position I held for the one year that was required to qualify for a scholarship to study in the United States. I was again fortunate that my husband supported my educational goals and aspirations and that he too qualified for a scholarship to study in the U.S.; had he not qualified, I would not have been allowed to travel overseas alone to study.

We chose to study at Utah State University but when I arrived in America, I had two problems: first, I couldn't speak English well enough for graduate-level study and secondly, I didn't know what to study. Intensive language study solved my first problem.

My second problem was solved by accident when a Palestinian friend in Utah advised me to look into a new major that was being offered at Utah State, which was "Instructional Technology." I was unsure about it and questioned whether I could find employment back home with such a degree. Nevertheless, I followed my friend's advice and studied instructional technology.

I look back upon my time in Utah with fond memories. I socialized freely in the broader society and also within the rather large Arabic speaking community. By the time we returned to Saudi Arabia I was fluent in English.

After returning to Saudi Arabia in 1983 with two children, I was employed as a manager and instructor at the Institute of Public Administration (IPA). My skills were tapped to design and deliver training programs for women in the women's branch of the IPA. Finally, things began to get interesting in my career and I was able to move beyond the question of "what should I be" to "what shall I do to make a difference?"

Making a Difference

No matter what difference we as individuals seek to make in our respective disciplines, to be effective we must make such differences within the context of what's appropriate at that time within our society. Accordingly, in order to move the girls' education agenda forward and to implement educational technology in the process, enabling and facilitating policies were required that conformed to the Saudi context. The ground was laid for this by placing a greater emphasis on the use of instructional technology in both the Third (1980–1985) and Fourth (1985–1990) National Development Plans. In addition to this policy framework, what was also needed was the belief and enthusiasm of teachers about the usefulness of audiovisual and other technological aids as an alternative and/or facilitative means of instruction. It was my job to be an advocate for these modern interventions and tools and to encourage teachers to embrace them.

Another key dimension of my job was to be an advocate for the use of technology to address and serve those with special needs in our society. I believed in the utility of technology for such purposes and I dedicated the next four years of my work to serving this constituency as the "Teaching Aids Supervisor" for the Special Needs Center within the Ministry of Education. What I learned from this experience is that while supportive education policies matter, perhaps what matters most is a positive attitude and the commitment to making a difference.

When I think back to my early pondering about what to be when I grew up, it is now clear that what I was supposed to do is precisely what I am doing: advocating for inclusive education for students with disabilities and demonstrating the importance of leveraging technology in educating special needs students. Had my friend in Utah not steered me in the direction of studying instructional technology I might have missed out on this wonderful opportunity to help those with special needs.

Striking While the Iron is Hot

When I step back and reflect on what has happened over the past four decades with respect to the education of females and the changes within our society as a whole, I am astounded. The snapshot doesn't render a photo that is the same as in the west; rather, it is a moving picture that is changing all the time. Formal education for girls was established not long after I was born and since then there have been many milestones along the way.

Today, Saudi Arabia provides female students with one of the world's largest scholarship programs and, as a result, thousands of women have earned master's degrees and doctorates from international universities. Today, women make up over 56% of enrollment at universities in Saudi Arabia. Additionally, Princess Norah bint Abdul Rahman University (PNU), the first women's university in Saudi Arabia, is the largest women's university in the world with 32 campuses across the Riyadh region.

There have been various criticisms of the Saudi education system over time and some of these criticisms have been addressed. However, one positive constant is that the Kingdom remains committed to continual improvement of the educational system. For instance, one of the main external criticisms of the Saudi educational curricula has been its focus on memorization. The government responded to this by implementing a series of initiatives to enhance the learning experience and improve the quality of education, such as the King Abdullah bin Abdul Aziz Al Saud Project for General Education Development (Tatweer). The project's main objectives are to introduce positive changes to the Saudi education system to help students gain knowledge and expertise, to train teachers, and to apply modern technology to enhance teaching and learning outcomes across the Kingdom.

Indeed, my own appointment as the then-highest ranking female member of the government has been heralded as a giant leap forward and demonstrative of the government's commitment to advancing girls' education. In a short time since my appointment, I was able to oversee and implement curriculum revisions and enhancements, craft professional development and support programs for teachers, create professional learning communities and support community engagement in extracurricular activities, to name a few of my initiatives.

I knew immediately upon being appointed that I had to strike while the iron was hot. In addition to the changes I instituted described earlier, I actively supported several specific initiatives. The first was in the area of early childhood education where we expanded the number of kindergartens from 500 to 1,591 in three years. Secondly, in the area of early childhood education, a key initiative was the development of Saudi Early Learning Standards (SELS), which was developed by an elite group of early childhood education leaders from the Ministry of Education, the National Association for Education of Young Children (NAEYC), and teams of specialists under the supervision of Tatweer. This fruitful collaborative of early childhood education leaders and specialists has contributed to the establishment of comprehensive national standards for the early childhood stage of education, not only for the Kingdom but also for the Arab and Islamic world. To take this success a step further and to compliment the SELS, I also supported the development of a revised early childhood education curriculum along with intensive professional development programs for early childhood education teachers.

Opportunities abound in the education ministry to make a difference and, for my part, I have tried to seize as many as possible as quickly as possible. One such area for immediate action is the expansion of days care centers, especially catering to children from 1 month to 3 years old. Increasing the number of day care centers is important because having them enables more women to feel free to get out and work and thereby utilize the education they have attained.

Another area that I have prioritized is improving access to education for students with special needs, which is clearly close to my heart given my previous tenure at IPA. I have also prioritized helping women gain experience to become decision makers. This goal is consistent with one of the directives of Ninth National Development Plan, which is to promote improvements in the status of women and also to enable them to participate in the development of the country. While the Plan includes objectives and policies that address issues relevant to the development of women's status in various areas, foremost is education. In terms of women's leadership within education, the appointment of Dr. Haya Al Awad as a deputy minister for girls' education and the appointment of more than 56 other females in leadership positions demonstrates that progress is being made.

Changing Times

Although the public provision of education for girls in Saudi Arabia started after boys, it achieved parity on all fronts by 2001. Last year, the number of schools for girls outnumbered that for boys, and the number of girls enrolled in public schools is over two million, which is only slightly behind the number of boys.

When I was diagnosed with cancer, five years after being appointed to my current position, I had to go to the United States for surgery. This was not a set-back for me; in fact, it strengthened my resolve to move with great speed in getting my job done and to continue making a difference.

When people look at what we have accomplished as women in Saudi Arabia since being given the opportunity to become educated, they can't help but conclude that we have made great strides in a short time. Saudi women are now lawyers, engineers, scientists, bankers and successful businesswoman, and there are also 30 women on the consultative Shura Council (making up 20% of the appointees). Such change began a number of years ago, and today education and opportunities for women in the great Kingdom of Saudi Arabia continue to evolve at an ever quickening pace.

Although I am no longer the Vice Minister for Girls' Education, I am still actively engaged as an Advisor to the Ministry and, most importantly, I remain an advocate for the education and advancement of women.

About
Banyan Mohmoud Al-Zahran

In 2013 Bayan Mahmoud Al-Zahran became the first woman licensed to practice law in Saudi Arabia, and in 2014, she opened the Kingdom's first-ever all-woman law firm. She became the first female lawyer to defend a client in 2014 when she appeared in the General Court in Jeddah.

Conditions to obtain the license are the same for men and women and include a university degree in law and three years of training. The initial plan of the Saudi justice ministry was to allocate licenses to females to handle family status cases, but the final decision did not impose any limits on fields of law practice. Without any imposed limits, Al-Zahran and her firm of all female lawyers represent both men and women. One of the firm's stated goals, however, is to argue cases on behalf of Saudi women in court and to fight for the rights of local women; in so doing, she help courts understand legal disputes from a female perspective.

Al-Zahran had been working as a legal consultant for several years before she was allowed to become a fully licensed lawyer in 2014, along with three other women, Jihan Qurban, Sara Al Omarri, and Ameera Quqani.

Al-Zahran, and her Jeddah-based all-female law firm, is contributing a lot to the legal system. Her firm is making a difference in the history of court cases and female disputes in the Kingdom, and importantly, Al-Zahran's example is showing the way for other female lawyers to follow. ❧

Banyan Mohmoud Al-Zahran

First Female Licensed Lawyer and
First Female Owner of a Law Firm

"Advancing Confidently in the Direction of Change"

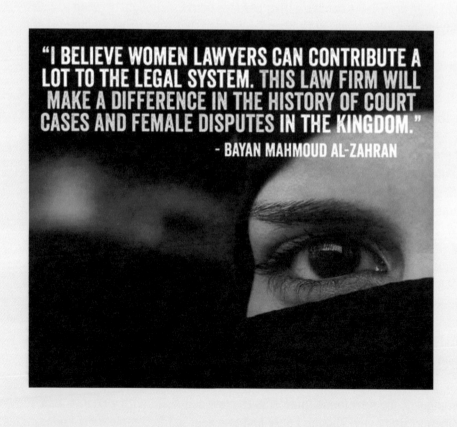

"I BELIEVE WOMEN LAWYERS CAN CONTRIBUTE A LOT TO THE LEGAL SYSTEM. THIS LAW FIRM WILL MAKE A DIFFERENCE IN THE HISTORY OF COURT CASES AND FEMALE DISPUTES IN THE KINGDOM."
- BAYAN MAHMOUD AL-ZAHRAN

Early Life

Thirty years ago when I was born, who would have thought it would be possible to be a licensed female lawyer in Saudi Arabia? I, for one, never considered this prospect. How could I even imagine something like that? I didn't have any information at my disposal that would have led me in that direction, or so I thought.

From my optic, the law and the entire legal process were behind a veil. I didn't come from a family of lawyers and I knew nothing about the inner workings of the law. The spark had to come from the outside.

Like most Saudi mothers thirty years ago, mine was uneducated, which doesn't mean that she didn't impart valuable lessons and support my development. While my mother did these things, it was my father – a professional actively engaged in society – who I looked up to and relied upon him for career advice. Beyond merely seeking his advice, I wanted to emulate my father and follow in his footsteps. He was a businessman so I wanted to be a businesswoman. It followed that I should study business in college.

Had I been born just a decade earlier perhaps both the thought of going to college and studying business would have been far-fetched, but sometimes timing is everything.

An Eye Opener

Although I was married at 16 years old I went on to attend university, where I studied business administration. During the third year of my studies, fate intervened. I was on holiday with my friend when she developed a medical problem. It turned out the problem was caused by a doctor. In order to help her, I researched medical  malpractice on the internet. The more I researched, the more fascinated I became with the subject of law.

Fortuitously, my new found interest in the law coincided with a change that allowed women to study law. Though I only had one year left to complete my undergraduate studies in business, I immediately changed my focus to study law. Although this change entailed three additional years of study, I didn't mind because I believed that studying law was my true destiny. Perhaps the other thirty four girls who also chose to study law in this first ever graduating class felt similarly.

We didn't know what we would do after studying law but in case societal change occurred, we would be prepared and willing to serve.

Eyes Wide Open; Doors Firmly Shut

In 2009, we did it; we were the first female law graduates in the history of Saudi Arabia. So what's next, we all wondered? If there was a master plan the leaders of the country had about what female law graduates would be permitted to do with their law degrees, no one told us about that.

Despite this uncertainty, I felt emboldened by my law degree and my newly acquired knowledge. I even got up the nerve to approach various law firms in Jeddah for employment but, alas, they weren't as bold. Time after time the answer was the same: No females allowed.

Taking stock of my situation, I considered my position: One law degree, no license, no job and no experience in or exposure to the court system. What, I wondered, could I do?

Then it hit me: No one was stopping me from volunteering. In fact, the solution was right in front of me but I couldn't see it. My father had established a shelter for abused women, so perhaps I could help these women in some way.

I give my father credit for supporting me in volunteering and helping me find my way. Neither of us knew if I'd ever be able to practice law as a licensed attorney but there were certainly many opportunities to provide valuable advice and counsel to these women in the shelter, whether I had a license or not.

Quid Pro Quo: I helped the Women and the Women Helped Me

To understand the situation of women in Saudi Arabia and why some are in dire need of legal assistance, one must first understand a few issues concerning the traditions in the society and how the society has evolved.

It's a complicated story, no doubt, and not easy to explain. However, there are a few things to that should be explained to provide a bit of a context. The first is that it wasn't until the 21st century that a woman could have her own identity, literally. Before that, women were not issued identification (ID) cards but rather were named as dependents on their mahram's (any relative that a Muslim is not allowed to marry is mahram; usually their father or husband) ID card, so in effect women were not allowed in public without their mahram.

Without ID cards, proving you were who you said you were in the court system was a challenge for Saudi women. Absent an ID card, passport or driver's license, women had to produce two male relations to confirm their identity. If a man denied that the woman in court was his mother/sister/daughter, the man's word would normally be accepted, making a woman vulnerable to false claims to her property and other violations.

The first ID cards were issued in 2001 and only to women who had permission from their mahram - but even then these cards were issued to the mahram, not to the women. 2006 marked a giant leap forward when the mahram's permission was no longer required. And in 2013, ID cards became compulsory for women. The cards include GPS tracking, fingerprints, and other features that make them difficult to forge; and while women do not need male permission to apply for ID cards, they do need it to travel abroad.

Granting ID cards to females was a hard-won battle. The Ulama, Saudi's religious authorities, fiercely opposed the idea of issuing separate identity cards for women, arguing that cards showing a woman's unveiled face violate purdah (a religious practice of female seclusion that may include physical segregation behind walls and concealing garments) and Saudi custom.

The treatment of issues pertaining to child custody and domestic violence, for instance, are also important to understand as such treatment often places women at a disadvantage.

When it comes to child custody, children belong to their father, who has sole guardianship. If a couple divorces, the woman may be granted custody of her young children until they reach the age of seven. Older children are often awarded to the father or the paternal grandparents, and under no circumstance can a woman confer citizenship to children born to a non-Saudi Arabian father.

Tackling the issue of domestic violence is one of the new frontiers that has seen significant societal change. In a landmark decision in August 2013, the Saudi cabinet approved a law making domestic violence a criminal offence for the first time, calling for up to a year in prison and a fine, with double the consequences for repeat offenders. The law criminalizes psychological and sexual abuse as well as physical abuse. Before this law was passed, violence against women and children in the home was not traditionally considered a criminal matter. Today, women still fall prey to misfortunes and require legal advice, and this is where my law firm can provide assistance.

You Have Me and I have You: Together We Will Make Justice Happen

I had never stepped foot inside a court room and nothing in my studies had prepared me for court proceedings. As a woman, I was reduced to being mere moral support, accompanying the women I was assisting.

During those initial court proceedings, I listened well and learned little by little. In the eyes of the court, I was permitted to accompany the women as their "friend."

Over the years there would be many "friends." Gradually, I gained a reputation as a "friend" of the poor, all the while gleaning valuable lessons learned each time I was in court.

In addition to helping the women in the shelter, I also volunteered from 2009 to 2011 with a foundation devoted to protecting families and acquired the title of "consultant" to the foundation. Being able to be referred to as a "consultant" as opposed to merely a "friend" was a major step forward. Even so, I had to present a letter to the court verifying that I was "retained" as a consultant. In total, I was involved in about 40 cases and each one taught me a lot.

Armed with the knowledge and experience of my years as a "friend" and "consultant" to the downtrodden, I qualified myself to practice law.

Continuing in my "self-qualification process" after two years of helping women in the shelter, I branched out and began volunteering for another foundation that focused on caring for the families of prisoners and for prisoners after their release. This too was an experience where I could learn a lot, especially as some crimes and their punishments are clear in the Saudi system while others are not.

In the latter category are modern crimes not foreseen in the Quran like drug trafficking or the possession and use of weapons. Such modern crimes give great autonomy to judges, who are trained in Shariah law but not bound by judicial precedent, to define crimes and to issue punishments according to their judgments. Experience in seeing how justice is levied in such cases was invaluable.

The Key to Opening the Door

By 2011, the time had come for female law graduates to take a stand. Where was it written that that law degree holding females shouldn't practice law? So, about 100 female law graduates and I banded together and plotted the way forward—and there was only one way forward: To prove unequivocally that there was nothing in the Quran that prohibited women from practicing law. This was the key to opening the door. All judges in Saudi Arabia are required to attend religious school and are trained in Shariah law; if we based our case on a thorough understanding of this law, we would be able to "speak into their listening" and win the day.

It took all 100 of us over two years to undertake the research necessary to make our case. Indeed, we proved without a shadow of a doubt that nothing in the Quran was against women practicing law.

We won and in 2013, I became the first female in the history of Saudi Arabia to be granted a license to practice law. This was not only my victory; it was a victory for the women of Saudi Arabia.

As a licensed lawyer, I now have the opportunity to formally represent women and others in need and in so doing to understand their plights with the compassion and empathy their cases warrant.

At the end of the day, it's all about empathy. All of those years going to the courts, hearing the trials of the women who needed shelter and the families of the imprisoned as a "friend" of the poor, indeed deepened my well of empathy and my resolve to help them seek justice.

Does it matter that I am a female lawyer? I believe that it does; my female clients appreciate that I'm on their side and that they can "speak into my listening."

Hanging Out My Shingle

There are three reasons why I decided to "hang out my shingle" and establish my own law firm. The first is that none of my male colleagues dared to hire or collaborate with me. Secondly, I felt qualified and knew that there was a constituency out there who needed me. Finally, it occurred to me that as my first intended love was business, why couldn't I combine business and the practice of law into the practice of law as a business?

Admittedly, establishing my office was not easy. It took more than six months and required me to jump through all kinds of hurdles, including securing the assets to be self-financed.

What a glorious day it was when my office finally opened. My father officiated, my mother cut the ribbon, my husband celebrated and my two children cheered me on.

Saudi Arabia is evolving constantly, and I see myself as both a symbol of that evolution and as an active contributor to its continuance.

Open for Business

January 2014

Bayan Mahmoud Al-Zahran the First Saudi Female Law Firm

The first all-female law practice has opened in Saudi Arabia, marking progress for women in a nation that has historically not afforded even many basic rights to women.

Bayan Mahmoud Al-Zahran, the first woman in Saudi Arabia to be issued a law license, along with Jihan Qurban, Sarra al-Omari and Ameera Quqani, opened the firm on January 1, 2014. While they will provide services for both genders, the stated objective of the new law firm is to advocate for the rights of Saudi women and to bring cases centered on women to court.

Al-Zahran officially became Saudi Arabia's first female lawyer on November 2013 when she defended a client at the General Court in Jeddah. She had worked for many years as a legal consultant, the only legal position previously open to women, and had represented clients in dozens of court cases.

In a strictly sex-segregated society such as Saudi Arabia, it can be hard for men and women to speak openly and understand the issues put forth by an opposite-sex client, she says.

With more female lawyers in Saudi Arabia, this hurdle for women could be alleviated.

Al-Zahran asserts, "I believe women lawyers can contribute a lot to the legal system. This law firm will make a difference in the history of court cases and female disputes in the Kingdom. I am very hopeful..."

She also states her desire for the number of female lawyers to rise in the future.

At the opening of the firm, the vice president of the Jeddah Chamber of Commerce, Mazen Batterjee, congratulated the new lawyers, but cautioned them to remain true to Sharia law in their practice and in their personal lives. He reiterated that the women should always wear their hijabs to court.

Batterjee's tentative praise and caution are outshined by the enthusiasm of Al-Zahran's father, Sheikh Mahmoud.

He calls the move an important step for women's rights and affirmed his complete support his daughter. "We are very proud of our daughter who stands firm for [the] protection of women's rights," he states.

The issue of women's rights in Saudi Arabia has long been a contentious one.

Women living in the Kingdom still must have a male guardian who can decide if a woman can travel, work, marry or go to school—for their entire lives.

Women are also expected to fully cover themselves in public spaces and are forbidden from driving.

In October 2013, over 60 women drove cars in protest of the law, a move that earned global attention and praise while pointing to a growing, though still small, movement in Saudi Arabia toward increased rights for women.

If it is up to her and her firm's lawyers, Al-Zahran plans to see the dream of women rights in Saudi Arabia fully realized.

I know that some of our traditions and systems in Saudi Arabia are complicated, but I'm hopeful that by understanding them and working through them, we can nevertheless help those in need obtain the justice they deserve. Beyond being hopeful though, I have actually seen proof that this is possible and am myself part of that proof. By demonstrating that practicing law as a woman was not inconsistent with the Quran and Shariah law, women were granted the right to practice it. This underscores the importance of working through the system instead of against it. As a dedicated Muslim, I believe in the goodness and light of our religion, and its ability to form the basis of our law and to render just results. As a lawyer, it's my duty and obligation to find the right arguments upon which we can all agree that renders the desired outcomes.

With regard to the pace of change in our society, I see both positive movements forward and evidence of taking steps backward – but on balance I can say the positive outweighs the negative. For women, I see many reassuring and positive signs of progress such as the recent appointment of the first female Vice Minister of Education, the appointment to women to the Shura Council and other positive steps including granting me my attorney's license.

As for my own law practice, I am pleased to say that we are growing; we're in fact moving to bigger offices just after one year in service and have added five new lawyers. There is an appetite for female legal representation not only from women but from others in society who trust that female lawyers can add a dimension to legal representation that prioritizes both competence and empathy. We stand ready to meet their needs and are open for business.

About
Huda Abdul Rahman Ali Al-Jeraisy

Huda Al-Jeraisy is a businesswoman and leader within the women's wing of the Riyadh Chamber of Commerce and Industry (RCCI). The women's section acts as a mini-Chamber of Commerce and offers women information and services to promote their entrepreneurship.

Huda's own private sector experience began in 1992 when she was a supervisor in a women's computer training center. She went on to become the manager of the center and is today its owner. It is the Asr Al-Areeba for Ladies Skills, which provides training to women in a variety of sectors.

Huda holds a B.A in Translation from Geneva University in Switzerland, where she studied French, English, and Arabic. Prior to studying in Switzerland, she lived in Lebanon where she studied in the early grades. As a continuing learner, she has taken courses in many subject areas such as computer science, management, leadership, and business administration, among others, which keeps her abreast of subjects of relevance to her women's training center.

Huda is widely known for her volunteer work. She has served as a member of different committees within the Riyadh Chamber of Commerce & Industry (RCCI), the Ministry of Education, the Disabled Children Association, the Saudi Association for Media and Communication, the Riyadh Economic Forum, the Council of Saudi Chambers of Commerce and Industry, the Ministry of Labor, and the King Saud University. Her focus has been to advocate for the expanded economic and civic participation of women.

Huda has also been actively engaged in politics within the Riyadh Chamber of Commerce & Industry (RCCI) and twice nominated herself for the Board of Directors of the Riyadh Chamber.

Her work and advocacy on behalf of women's economic participation was recognized internationally when then French President Nicolas Sarkozy awarded Huda Al-Jeraisy, Chairwoman of the Executive Council in the Women's Section at the Riyadh Chamber of Commerce and Industry (RCCI), the medal "Baroness in the Order of the Legion of Honor" in 2011 to recognize her efforts and contributions toward strengthening economic and investment relations between Saudi Arabia and France. Upon receiving the award, Huda commented: "…that the medal was also an honor for her female colleagues in the Women's Section of the RCCI and for all businesswomen in the Kingdom." ✤

Huda Al-Jeraisy

Chairwoman of the Women's Committee
Council of Saudi Chambers

Chairwoman, Executive Women's Council
Riyadh Chamber of Commerce & Industry

"Overcoming Life's Challenges"

Early Life

Most of us eventually confront our inner brick wall and when we do our choice is to break it or give up and fall.

I shattered my brick wall at a very young age. When I was four months old, I contracted polio. At the time, facilities weren't available in Saudi Arabia to attend to my medical needs so my father took me to Lebanon to a hospital where I remained until I was 14 years old. My choice was clear: Break through the wall, or give up and fall. I chose to break through. Today, I walk with crutches but I am walking – and I'm certainly talking a lot, just ask my colleagues.

Growing up in a hospital makes you see the world differently, and perhaps more empathetically. Indeed, there were a lot of "understandings" I had to come to grips with early on, starting with my own situation and then with the world around me.

Fortunately, I had my "regular family" back in Saudi Arabia, who so lovingly visited me every summer, and I had my "hospital family" with whom I lived on a daily basis. I also had my siblings from my mother and those from my father's second family. In short, I was away from home but not alone. All the while, it was up to me to search for and tap into my inner strength deep inside because from my obstacles I could not hide.

Embracing Challenges

As they say, we must embrace and defeat our challenges so that we can open the door and greet our true purpose.

After living with my hospital family for over 13 years in Lebanon, the time had come to return to Saudi Arabia, but I didn't know it. I thought I was going to Saudi Arabia for vacation just for a short while after the civil war in Lebanon broke out. I was expecting to return to Lebanon to continue my studies and treatment but the war continued to rage on.

This is when I had to come face to face with my new reality. Growing up in Lebanon had set me apart from girls my age that grew up in Saudi Arabia. Unlike them, I grew up in a non-male-female segregated environment. In addition, though I lived in a hospital, I went to a private school during the day and returned to the hospital afterwards. Significantly, I was the only handicapped person in the private school I attended, as it was not a school for handicapped children. Had it not been for the breakout of war in Lebanon, I would have stayed in Lebanon to attend high school but, when the war broke out, I had no choice but to return to Saudi Arabia.

The adjustment to Saudi Arabia was very difficult and I wasn't happy, to put it mildly. I heard the many whispers, "Oh, poor girl," and I didn't like it. Despite my physical ailments, I didn't think of myself in the terms I was being viewed. To me, when all we see is darkness and gloom we are destined to keep running from the gloom.

I refused to view myself as pitiful or the world as gloomy, but I did need time to brace and adjust myself to my new reality. I really wanted to go back to Lebanon but, alas, it wasn't possible. My father saw that I wasn't happy so he took me to Lausanne, Switzerland, to attend high school there.

The move to Switzerland turned out to be a very good one for me. Its educational system required students to add a language each couple of years in the course of study. For me, first there was French, then English and then Italian...and voilà, I discovered a career path. I would go on to study language translation at the university level in Geneva, Switzerland.

Calculating the Cost of Non Conformity

Life is full of equations. How many steps will it take to cross the street; how many coins will it take to purchase something; how many days until vacation…etc. Some of these calculations are simple and benign – but some are decidedly not.

My mother, my role model, had to make a very important calculation early in her  life. She was very unhappy that my father took another wife and set up another household. Yes, it was allowed under the law but that doesn't mean she welcomed or liked it. She had to make a choice: Leave him and return to her father's house, her only other option, or grin and bear it. In her wisdom, she chose the latter. After all, she had five small children.

I too had an important choice to make when I returned to Saudi Arabia: To veil or not to veil?

I wasn't used to wearing a veil and, frankly, I didn't want to. I soon learned, however, that in Saudi Arabia it's best to fall in line.

At first, I tried to use my handicap to suggest that wearing a veil would impair my mobility. Yes, I could sort of get away with it but, at the end of the day, I learned that if you really want to achieve your goals, it's best to work within the society rather than outside of it. Not wearing a veil here sends a message – and it's not a message that helps you win.

Once I understood that it's best to work within the system, my next challenge was to understand exactly how to do that.

First, there was the matter of my arranged marriage four years after I completed university in 1988. I fell in line. My only condition was that we respect each other and treat each other as equals. This was a lofty goal, it turns out. In the early years of our marriage, my husband didn't want me to accept outside engagements and I had to obey him and decline engagements until he finally came around. As time passed, he came to understand the importance of my work and decided to support it. Now, he tells our three children: "Children, your mother has to go out, she has important things to do." Indeed, we have come a long way, and I'm proud that my husband has evolved and become my great supporter.

Working Inside the Tent

With my relatively late in life acceptance of the fact that I needed to work within the norms and traditions of the society, I was almost ready to take on my life's work. First, however, I was employed as a translator in the Women's Employment Office in the Ministry of Civil Service for one year after I graduated from Geneva

University in Switzerland with an undergraduate degree in language translation. Back then, working in the public service was one of the few options for employment for women. My job was not satisfying. I was supposed to be a translator but I was given little to translate. I was bored and tried to gain experience by helping in different departments, but finally I decided to move on.

On reflection, however, I realize that my employment served to deepen my understanding of how things worked in the Kingdom, especially with respect to the segregation of males and females. My job was essentially a training ground for learning about Saudi Arabia and the position of women in it. I was further enlightened by my work over the next two years with the National Research Center as an International News Analyst. It gave me a perspective about how the world views Saudi Arabia and vice versa. At the end of the day, however, it was also uninspiring work because there was no room for creativity.

It turns out my true calling was business. My father had always wanted me to be independent and I realized that the path to independence for me was entrepreneurship. My father is a businessman who sells equipment and furniture. Through his position as President of the Riyadh Chamber of Commerce, he helped pave the way for me to become independent in business and to establish myself with the Chamber.

It wasn't easy entering the Chamber of Commerce's "tent" as a woman. Just as tents are upheld by stakes in the ground, the women of Saudi Arabia have significant economic stakes in the country's future, and must be engaged in holding up the Chamber's tent.

As for my own stake in the economy, I started out in the private sector working as a supervisor in various departments in a women's computer training center. Eventually, I worked my way up to the manager's position and finally to being the owner of "Al Areeba for Ladies Skills Center," a vocational training and recruitment center in Riyadh.

Owning a Business and Running a Business Are Two Different Things

To be clear, there are a number of Saudi Arabian women who are business owners. The issue is whether they are able to actually run the businesses they own.

Some women are thrust into business ownership as heirs to family-owned businesses and/or as partial owners of family run businesses. Because of this, as required under Shariah inheritance law (Islamic law), many women own considerable fortunes in their own right and also comprise a good amount of the Kingdom's wealth. Such business ownership means that women have substantial assets in real estate, jewelry, precious stones and metals. To be actively engaged in the management and operation of these businesses, however, they have to have business skills, and that's where the services of my firm and others like it can help bridge the gap.

It's important for women to become active in business for a number of reasons. If women were allowed to take a greater part in the economy, they could contribute to solving problems of Saudi unemployment and "Saudization" (localizing various categories of labor and industries). Each year, the number of females who are educated in universities rises. Those who don't take advantage of their knowledge through entrepreneurship miss out on a significant opportunity.

The number of professions women can pursue in Saudi Arabia is still quite limited, which also limits the degree to which women can contribute to the economy and the wealth of the country. Historically, women have been expected to go into nursing, medicine, education, charitable activities or the public sector. Thus far, in private business, the banking sector has been the most advanced in training women. Some commercial banks now have women not just as managers of women's branches of the banks but also as divisional managers in bank headquarters. Significantly, there was a recent breakthrough for women in the legal profession; they can now practice law as licensed attorneys.

Historically, businesswomen who actively sought to run their own operations used to face challenges due to the traditional nature of Saudi society and legal restrictions. While women were allowed into the Chambers of Commerce, it was often easier to work through a male intermediary acting as their power of attorney to process documentation.

A lack of mobility also hindered the development of national women's groups, as it was difficult for women to travel to different regions to meet with their counterparts to exchange ideas and information and to encourage each other's aspirations.

Today, an obstacle that continues to hinder women in business is their lack of employment experience. As global experience shows, business ideas often spring from work experience; the greater the scope of work experience, the broader the foundation for future business development. To overcome this challenge, government institutions and the private sector, especially regional Chambers of Commerce, including the RCCI, are increasingly helping women learn and gain skills that can be leveraged for business development.

Widening the Tent

In 2003, a number of businesswomen within the Riyadh Chamber of Commerce and Industry (RCCI) formed a Cultural Committee to show the Riyadh community that we exist and that we deserve support. As a result, the RCCI established a businesswomen's section in 2004, recognizing the role women play in the Kingdom's economy. That same year, female members were for the first time allowed to vote for RCCI's board of directors.

My father, RCCI President Abdulrahman Al-Jeraisy, championed the establishment of the businesswomen's section. "The section," he would say, "will act as a mini chamber of commerce offering all the services provided by headquarters, to which it will be electronically connected, in order to provide the information needed to help Saudi women run their own businesses." At the time, there were approximately 5,000 businesswomen in Riyadh, who comprised 14.11 percent of the Kingdom's workforce and held about 20 per cent of Saudi investment funds assets.

Once the women's section was established I was among the women nominated for a position within the women's section. Based on an internal election between women members I was

elected Vice-Chairperson (2004), then Chairperson (2006) of the executive board of the RCCI women's branch. As a member of RCCI's executive council thus, I explained that one of the key services of the new women's section will be authentication of the paperwork necessary for the establishment of a new business and that it would also run training programs and organize seminars for women.

As a semi-government entity, the Ministry of Commerce can appoint six members to the chamber board. Appointing women to any of these slots is a major step forward, but when the chamber body elects women, it's a significant barometer of societal change and acceptance.

Make no mistake: It has been hard to break new ground and gain acceptance within the Chamber. In 2008, for instance, the major headlines pronounced:

> **"Women put up spirited fight in Riyadh chamber elections:** For the first time in the 50-year history of the Riyadh Chamber of Commerce and Industry, women candidates are putting up a tough challenge to their male counterparts in the election to the chamber's 12-member board of directors."

There were 37 candidates competing then for the 12 board seats, including three women: Myself and candidates Amal Badr Al Deen and Basima Qashma. Earlier, it's noted that women were elected and appointed to the board of directors of the chamber in Jeddah but only appointed, but not elected to the chamber board in Dammam.

It is also noteworthy that during the campaign, many of the male candidates employed technology to attract voters. "They managed to establish close contacts with some 41,000 voters through various means of communications such as direct contact, e-mail, SMS and fax, besides telephone calls." Because of their mobility, some of the male candidates were also able to visit the homes of some of the 41,000 members of the chamber and to meet with voters at the branches of the chamber in various parts of the city.

The female candidates did not win but it's notable that I got 778 votes—and most of them were from men. We were down, but not out and we refused to give up.

When At First You Don't Succeed, Try, Try Again

By 2012, there were over 80,000 members of the Riyadh Chamber and elections were held for the 16th session. At this point, my father had been the chairman since the 11th session in 1992. Many changes to the voting process had been made, many of which would presumably favor women. I threw my hat in the ring again but didn't secure enough votes to be elected to the board of directors.

This has not dampened my spirit or resolve to help empower women with the business skills they need to succeed in business.

Leaving politics aside, I have continued to do all that I can do to shine a path for women on the road to entrepreneurship.

In the face of some of the persisting licensing restrictions, I have been called upon to show women how to create some "workarounds" to expand their business horizons—and by the way, it's also worth mentioning that men also face hurdles in starting their businesses.

Women, however, face relatively more hurdles and require more assistance. For instance, I remember when a woman sought my advice on how to set up a tailoring training institute. In fact, at the time, it wasn't possible for a woman to get a license to conduct such a training institute. I explained that the closest approximation to a license for that purpose would be a license for computer training, which was permitted at the time. I gave her my already established IT curricula and walked her through the business formation process. She applied for a license to operate a computer training business and wound up actually opening a center for IT training instead of a center for tailoring training. As a result her new business was in direct competition with my IT training business, but I didn't care; it was more important to encourage other women to become entrepreneurs.

Little by little, through various means such as by royal decrees and private sector advocacy, things are beginning to open up for women, both in employment and in business. Oftentimes, the two are inextricably linked with the former laying the ground for the latter, as I have mentioned. A good example is what happened in 2012. It may seem like a small thing but it was a giant step in our societal context and it garnered major headlines news, not only in Saudi Arabia, but around the world. The news reported:

> "The Ministry of Labor is enforcing a royal decree issued last summer ordering that sales personnel in shops selling garments and other goods, like cosmetics, that are only for women must be female. More than 28,000 women applied for the jobs, the ministry said. Anywhere else in the world, it would not be news that sales assistants in shops selling panties and bras were female. In Saudi Arabia, where women have always been excluded from the public work force, it is a critical breakthrough. This is not just about intimate garments; this is a milestone on the arduous path to employment equality for women in a country where they are systematically excluded from retail activity."

The news also reported that "Saudi Arabia's economic planners recognize that if women are going to be educated at public expense, as they now are in increasing numbers, they will expect to work and the country will need their economic output."

Society has increasingly accepted the idea that women will work outside the home. They have long been employed in medicine and education. Today, retail commerce is a new frontier because such work usually requires interactions with men, which is prohibited, but ground is also being made in this area and now women are allowed to work in lingerie shops.

There's No Royal Flower-Strewn Path to Success for Women

Women in business have to want to succeed and fight for success and, when necessary, we must also break barriers to make success achievable.

Sometimes the sound of the barriers breaking is so loud that it's heard around the world, which is what happened when the French Government awarded me an honor in recognition of my work.

Of course, it feels good and is validating when one's work is acknowledged. My work, however, is not done. Saudi businesswomen are in the trenches, helping women prepare themselves to take advantage of technology and to learn the business skills they must acquire to be successful in business.

While I want to see women succeed as much as possible in business, I do not want us to lose our culture in the process. I remember how hard it was for me to fit myself into the culture when I returned to Saudi Arabia from Lebanon. Now, I tell my children: "Get your first degree in Saudi Arabia and get to know your culture and develop your networks on the inside before you go out."

As we continue to make strides to help empower women through our training efforts and through their inclusion at our chamber, we are mindful that while success is getting what you want, happiness is wanting what you get. We want to succeed within our culture, not outside of it.

My son Muhannad Al Badri and father Abdul Rahman Al-Jeraisy

Huda Al-Jeraisy honored by France

HAZIM AL-MUTAIRI

RIYADH: French President Nicolas Sarkozy has awarded Huda Al-Jeraisy, Chairwoman of the Executive Council in the Women's Section at the Riyadh Chamber of Commerce and Industry (RCCI), the medal "Baroness in the Order of the Legion of Honor". This is to recognize her efforts and contributions to strengthen economic and investment relations between Saudi Arabia and France.

Bertrand Besancenot, the French Ambassador to the Kingdom, informed Al-Jeraisy in a letter accompanying the medal, which was awarded after a recommendation from the embassy. He pointed out that the medal was awarded in terms of a decree issued on May 18.

Abdul Rahman Bin Ali Al-Jeraisy, Chairman of the Board of Directors of the RCCI, congratulated Al-Jeraisy on the honor. "It is part of our work to exert our utmost to boost cooperation and economic partnership between the Kingdom and different countries of the world, especially those that have big economies." The RCCI chairman said good economic relations with other countries are part of the plans of the leadership led by King Abdullah, Custodian of the Two Holy Mosques; the Crown Prince and the Second Deputy Premier.

Hussein Bin Abdul Rahman Al-Athel, Secretary General of the RCCI, was happy the award was given to Al-Jeraisy for her efforts to serve the businesswomen's sector and the Council of Saudi Chambers. He expressed his hope that her efforts would continue with the support and encouragement of the Kingdom's leadership. Al-Jeraisy said the medal was an honor and she was proud of being a Saudi citizen who has contributed to enhancement of cooperation and friendship between the Kingdom and France, one of the latter's biggest trade and investment partners.

She said the medal was also an honor for her female colleagues in the Women's Section of the RCCI and for all businesswomen in the Kingdom. Al-Jeraisy has been the chairwoman of the Executive Council of the Women's Section of the RCCI for several years now and is the first person to occupy this post since its inception.

– Okaz/Saudi Gazette

About
Dr. Madja Mohamed Ahmed Abu-Ras

Dr. Madja Abu-Ras is a Board Member and Deputy Executive Director of the Saudi Environmental Society (SEN). In her capacity at SEN, Dr. abu-Ras designs and delivers public awareness programs and campaigns on a national, local, and community level. She is at the forefront of conceiving ideas for new environmental programs that address the most pressing needs of society.

She received a Ph.D. in Environmental Studies and Biotechnology from Surrey University, England in 2009, where her research focus was the environmental effect of petroleum crude oil on soil in Saudi Arabia.

Dr. Abu-Ras was the first woman in Saudi Arabia to be selected for the Environmental Leadership Ambassador Program. Today, the Ambassador's program is a persuasive tool for promoting environmental awareness, as it involves actors, football players, Islamic scholars, and well-known personalities in Saudi society. As an Environmental advocate, Dr. Abu-Ras is particularly focused on raising environmental awareness among the younger generation and has been instrumental in advocating for including environmental awareness in school curricula.

In addition to being a trailblazing advocate, Dr. Abu-Ras is also a pioneer in the environmental biotechnology field and was the first Saudi female to get a fellowship in this discipline.

As a member of the staff of the Microbiology Department of the Faculty of Science of King Abdulaziz University, Dr. Abu-Ras lectures in microbiology, microbiological pollution, microorganism physiology, industrial microbiology, and ecological pollution.

She is a member of numerous civic and social organizations in Saudi Arabia such as the Jeddah Governorate Higher Female Committee, the Teba Association, the Al-Eman Association for Cancer Diseases, the National Research Center, Egypt, the King Fahd Research Center, the Saudi AIDS Society, and the Governorate Urban Observatory Council.

Dr. Abu-Ras was honored as a Fellow of the International Federation of Professional and Business Women, which is a worldwide organization committed to networking among and empowering women worldwide. ❧

Dr. Madjah Abu-Ras

Environmentalist

"Going Green Is Going In the Right Direction"

Early Life

I was born into a loving, warm, and supportive family in 1974 in the holy city of Mecca. Given the historical and religious significance of the holy city, its inhabitants tend to be conservative and conformist. Fortunately for me, my parents' faith and understanding of Islam led them to encourage me to become educated without limits. Their point of view and practice accorded with that of King

Abdullah who stressed that women in Islam's history have always been effective at home and at work, and therefore the role of women should not be sidelined. For my part, I pleased my parents by demonstrating my aptitude for science and by excelling in school. As an "A" student I was able to break new ground by being allowed to go to the only co-educational undergraduate school, King Abdulaziz City for Science and Technology (KACST)[1], to study microbiology.

I went on to pursue a Master's of Science in Microbiology and Bio-remediation, focused on organic pollution, and then earned my Ph.D. in "Biotechnology of Environmental Contaminants" from the University of Surrey in England.

---

[1] The King Abdulaziz City for Science and Technology was established in 1977 as the Saudi Arabian National Center for Science & Technology and renamed King Abdulaziz City for Science and Technology in 1985.

My Path to Environmentalism

I am the first Saudi woman to specialize in oil-contaminated soil treatment and people listen when I speak about the environmental crisis facing Saudi Arabia.

While I had an aptitude for the life sciences I hadn't yet developed a true passion for it until one day I saw a bird struggling for life in my garden. I was at first apprehensive about approaching the dying bird because it was during the time of the "bird flu." When the bird died

I called a government agency to ask how to dispose it of it but the man on the other end of the phone simply hung up on me. I asked my father, a manager with the Ministry of Oil who was knowledgeable about the Saudi government, where I could take the dead bird to be tested, but he wasn't sure whose responsibility it would be, presuming it would likely be the responsibility of the Ministry of Agriculture. I never got an answer. In the end, I wound up burying the poor little bird in the garden.

My experience with the bird in my garden made an impression on me. I began to wonder how concerned citizens could get involved in advocating for and protecting the environment if they didn't know how to work within the prevailing system?

It then dawned on me that the way to put my academic knowledge of the environment to good use and to pursue a topic I was becoming increasingly passionate about was to become a pro-environment champion in Saudi Arabia and to get others engaged in the cause as well, especially women. My passion stems from my belief that Saudi Arabia is facing an environmental crisis and I can't sit around and watch that happen. I took action and established a society to identify and advocate for solutions to some of our challenging environmental problems.

At first, I wanted my environmental advocacy society to be women-only but just as I began to articulate its goals I learned that another society with similar values was being created by the Presidency of Meteorology and Environment Protection, a government agency. The Saudi Environmental Society (SENS) was established in 2006. Prince Turki Bin Naser appointed me a founding member. Because the goals of SENS and those of my own society coincided, I decided not to work independently but instead joined forces with SENS. I subsequently became a member of SENS's board and was later appointed acting executive director.

I was able to realize one of my original goals soon after my appointment to the SENS board by developing the National Program for Environmental Awareness and Sustainable Development. Now both a formal and active part of SENS, the program raises awareness about environmental issues and advocates for robust environmental regulations throughout the economy.

Though I am an environmental scientist, I maintain that even if I wasn't I would want and expect my voice to be heard because I would still have a stake in the environment, just as all citizens have. While studying in England, for instance, I observed how environmental concerns are treated as personal concerns of individuals throughout all levels of the society, and I think that's a good thing. My vision is for all Saudi citizens to be similarly engaged, for them to think about the environment as belonging to them, and for them to desire to protect it just as they protect their other belongings.

The Environmental Context in Saudi Arabia

The issue of environmental protection is a major concern for Saudi Arabia, a major oil producer. Accordingly, Saudi Arabia ratified the International Convention for the Prevention of Pollution of the Sea by Oil of 1954 and its various amendments, and the International Convention on Civil Liability for Oil Pollution Damage of 1969 and its protocols.

Yet, it wasn't until 2001 that the first comprehensive Saudi Arabian national environmental legislation was enacted, and not until 2003 that its implementing regulations were published. Under the Regulation, the Presidency of Meteorology and Environment (the PME), an agency of the Ministry of Defense, is charged with the general supervision of environmental affairs in Saudi Arabia.

The legislation sets forth wide-ranging prohibitions against pollution and contamination of air, land and water, with particular emphasis on parties involved in services, industry, and other economic activities. Owners of "projects," which are defined as utilities and facilities that may have an effect on the environment, are required, prior to setting up a project, to undertake an environmental evaluation that must be approved by the PME. In addition to national environmental legislation there are also location-specific environment regulations and those that specifically pertain to Saudi Aramco's various oil-related operations.

These regulations and others focus primarily on environmental protection, which is of paramount importance. My advocacy, however, goes beyond environmental protection to promoting sustainable green practices by all actors within the society.

Developing Green Consciousness

I have always loved everything green, so you could say that I had a high level of "green consciousness" or a "high green IQ" from the very beginning. My studies developed my "green" knowledge and now, through my work as an Associate Professor at King Abdul Aziz University's Biotechnology Department, I can pass on my knowledge and share my passion for the environment with the next generation.

As a mother of four sons, I have a very strong personal stake in the next generation as well. I had my sons before earning my Ph.D. and, perhaps because of them, when I began my doctoral program my resolve, focus, and clarity of my mission was strengthened. Today, after having previously divorced, I am happily married to someone who is very supportive of my career and advocacy work; he is also a renowned lawyer who in a position to help me navigate the system in my advocacy.

Just as a tree has many roots at its foundation, to be an effective environmental advocate I also have to have many strong roots that shore up the foundation for my advocacy work on behalf of the green cause. The various positions I hold in Saudi

Arabia are part of my root structure, as are the international organizations to which I belong.

I currently serve as the Director of the Euro-Arab women program for environment development of the Switzerland-based Euro-Arab Environment Organization. It has been beneficial, teaching me how I can adapt lessons learned to the Saudi situation. For instance, I have seen how the organization tailors its messages, programs and workshops to appeal to the issues within women's domains and spheres of influence. Housewives and mothers can promote the environmental cause at home in their daily practices and through educating and upbringing children. Women academics and women business owners each have their own constituency, and so on.

Youth Going Green

I find that young people are the most interested and zealous about going green and we, as advocates, are trying to harness their energy and enthusiasm.

Recently, the Saudi Environmental Society signed an agreement with the Minister of Education to support the National Program for Environmental Awareness and Sustainable Development, which also aims to educate children from kindergarten through primary and intermediate levels about the importance of preserving the environment. The program includes courses for teachers to train them on how to embed environmental programs in different curricula without relying on teaching a course called "environmental studies" *per se*. This approach recognizes and underscores that there are ways to be environmentally conscious in all that we do. At present, as advocates we are concentrating our efforts on kindergarten and primary schools and so far have succeeded in introducing environmental awareness programs at 332 schools throughout the country.

In my view, the youth will be the ones to promote the green cause; we just need to support them.

By contrast, we know that many adults in our society have a basic awareness of environmental issues—I'd venture to say around 60 percent—but many aren't ready to translate their concerns into action or to take a stand. We need to convey to them that any small thing they do to protect the environment counts. Also small inactions count like not throwing waste into the street.

While Saudi Arabia has many environmental regulations, at the end of the day each human being has to have it in his or her own heart to act responsibly toward the environment. It is impossible to legislate feelings so what we are trying to do through our advocacy is to show people the light so that they can "feel" a need to become personally responsible for protecting the environment in their own small ways.

The Green Light Going Forward

I'm optimistic about raising awareness and commitment to environmental protection and sustainability in Saudi Arabia. I see the impact. Each year, more people are coming forward to express their interest in learning more about how they can protect the environment.

At SENS, we have big plans going forward and four main targets: the government, which is responsible for infrastructure and promulgating the laws and regulations in support of the environment; the private sector, which has an opportunity to green its operations; societies and NGOs; and individuals. Our advocacy is aimed toward showing each stakeholder how to be more effective in contributing to sustainability.

I'm particularly keen to work with women to enlist them in our cause because women have power—more than is understood. After all, Saudi Arabia is a family-oriented society and women are very influential at home. Therefore, the more women involved in environmental protection, the greener we will become.

There are many positive signposts that society is placing an increasingly higher value on going green. For instance, the Saudi Government launched an "Environmental Management Award" in 2011 to promote good environmental practices that are consistent with the teachings of Islam. The award, with three levels of monetary prizes, may be granted to individuals, groups, institutions, organizations, companies,

associations or even to governmental, and non-governmental organizations, which underscores that all actors within society have opportunities to "green" their actions. The award recognizes such actions along the continuum, from stimulating and guiding scientific research, to mobilizing efforts to create innovative scientific and practical solutions for the current and future environmental problem, to everyday advocacy efforts.

At present, I am actively engaged in getting 14 municipalities to sign onto our SENS goal of aiming for a maximum ratio of waste per person of 1.6 kilograms and to support recycling campaigns. In one of our campaigns we were able to collect and recycle 36 tons of waste in just eight days. We are on the move and it's looking better and greener by the day.

About
Marwah Mohammed Hamoud Bakri

Dr. Marwah Bakri, Dean of Female Students Academic Complex and a member of the Science Faculty of Jazan University in Saudi Arabia since 2011, obtained a Ph.D. in Medical Microbiology from Glasgow Caledonian University in Scotland in the United Kingdom in 2010. She also earned a Master's of Science in Medical Microbiology from London University's School of Hygiene and Tropical Medicine in 2003, and earned an undergraduate degree in 2000.

Dr. Bakri has participated many in national conferences and published a number of articles in accredited journals. She is a member of microbiology associations in the USA, and England and Scotland; she is also active in many civic, scientific, and women's organizations in Saudi Arabia.

In Europe, she discovered *Clostridium difficile* bacterium that was found in salads. She also discovered the new ways of how the fatal *difficile*bacteria are transferred from animals to humans in Scotland. She was also the first to discover a new type of difficile bacteria in the intestines of cats. She was the first to study, develop, and segment genetic research on the clostridium bacteria in collaboration with Scotland Central Laboratory. Her publications include. *"The Gulf Woman: Present Routes and Future Gates"*, and *"An Introduction to the Science of Medical Microbiology"* (in press).

On the occasion of the International Women's Day in 2012, Dr. Marwah Mohammed Hamoud Bakri was awarded the 11th Middle East Prize granted by the Middle East Excellence Award Institute of Datamatix. The award is annually bestowed upon pioneering leaders worldwide and is attended by high ranking regional and international VIPs. Dr. Bakri won the award for excellence in leadership and decisionmaking. She was nominated by experts and specialists in the Middle East using the international criteria of leadership. It was noted at the time that the award was bestowed that…"it was very timely since Saudi Arabia had provided women a better atmosphere for innovation and scientific development especially under the umbrella of excellent strategy for learning and higher education instilled and implemented by the wise leadership of King Abdulla Bin Abdul Aziz, Custodian of the Two Holy Mosques." ❧

Dr. Marwah Bakri

Dean Female Students

Jazan University

"Searching for Answers"

Early Life

I grew up in Jazan, a port city and capital of the Jizan Region that lies in the southwest corner of Saudi Arabia north of the border with Yemen. Situated on the coast of the Red Sea it has historically served as an agricultural heartland and is noted for its high quality production of tropical fruits like mangoes, figs, and papaya. In the early 20th-century Jazan was a major site for pearl fishing but when World War I began trade declined at Jazan. From that time onward Jazan suffered and eventually became the poorest area in Saudi Arabia, with at least one third of the population living in poverty.

Jazan has a very hot desert climate and things typically move slowly. My childhood followed suit and the normal path for girls; I got married while I was still in high school and had my first child, a daughter, while I was still in high school. I was not expecting to have an extraordinary life.

My mother wanted me to go beyond the ordinary, however, but how I was supposed to accomplish that feat was unknown. Just because you may have aspirations doesn't mean you know your destination. Nevertheless, my mother helped me to prepare for the wishful journey to "somewhere unknown" by encouraging me to study; she awakened me each morning at 4 am for the purpose. No one had done that for her; she was illiterate and her mother had died when she was five years old. Though my father was a manager of Saudi Airlines in Nigeria, my mother knew little of the world upon which to base her encouragement of me. I did as my mother wanted and studied very hard. My relentless studying paid off. When my husband Zaki got accepted to Glasgow Caledonian in Scotland, I too was accepted and away we went.

Questions Without Answers

My husband and I were both progressing in our studies at university when we took a vacation to Spain. Our daughter fell ill while there so we aborted our vacation and immediately flew back to Glasgow to take her to the public hospital. At first, they said that there was no problem so we took her home. Within two days she fell terribly ill again; we took her back to the hospital but she grew yet worse while there. Many tests were performed, including an endoscopy (a procedure that examines the esophagus, stomach, and duodenum to detect gastrointestinal and digestive disorders). As our daughter's health was deteriorating before our very eyes we intervened to try to change the course of events by arranging for a private room and calling in private doctors. At one point there were seven doctors in the room conferring all at once.

We were overcome with grief and disbelief. We were supposed to be in one of the best hospitals in Europe, with the finest doctors and yet our daughter could not be saved. We didn't even know what she had contracted to have made her so violently ill in the first place.

The dreaded moment came to receive the news no parent would ever want to hear: Our beloved daughter had contracted a resistant form of bacteria in her blood and there was no hope. They said she was brain dead.

In the last moments I went to her at her bedside and whispered "Shahada" (surrender to him). I told her not to be afraid. I combed her hair, told her to be a good girl, and put her toys beside her.

We were in shock. Over the period of seven days we had lost our daughter, our only child; she was five years old and I was twenty one. I suddenly realized that in many ways I was a child myself, but my childhood came to an end the day my daughter died.

In Search of Answers

I vowed to find the answer to the mystery of my daughter's death, whatever it took. Though I had been studying computer science I decided to switch my field of study to biology believing that if I studied hard enough I could one day understand what had caused our daughter's death.

At first the university didn't agree to allow me to change my major; after all, I had not studied the prerequisite courses and for that matter I was not fully fluent in English. I appealed to their humanity though explaining what had happened to my daughter and that I was on a mission of discovery to understand what happened to her. I pleaded with the university officials and finally they had mercy on me and let me enroll in biology.

When I got a B+ in my microbiology course I considered it a gift from Allah. I was determined to learn all that I could to unveil the truth of what happened to my daughter. Who knew that my mother's constant prodding of me to study would lay the training ground for me to rise to this moment?

I thank my husband Zaki who gave me the space and time to fully devote myself to my studies. He also helped me study, as he too was studying science. He quizzed me over and over, made the dinner and did the chores. As mine was a much steeper uphill climb academically, my husband spared no effort to help me succeed. In short, my success is due in large part to him.

One thing I learned in the process is that it's one thing to aimlessly study but it's another to purposefully study. I was studying for a cause and I knew where I needed to land in my studies; I had to find a particular answer. What kind of bacteria caused my daughter to die and how had she contracted it? I wouldn't give up until I knew.

When Dedication and Perseverance Pays Off

Quite amazingly, a child bride from a poor area in Saudi Arabia, who was not fully fluent in English succeeded in unraveling one of the great medical mysteries in the public health system in Europe.

It took many hours of dedicated study—too many to count and too many days to enumerate but my passion to discover the source of bacteria that took our daughter propelled me in the right direction and I discovered *Clostridium difficile* bacterium and how the fatal *difficile* bacteria are transferred from animals to humans in Scotland.

In brief, *Clostridium difficile (C. Difficile)* colitis or "pseudomembranous colitis" is colitis (inflammation of the large intestine) that results from infection with *Clostridium difficile*, a type of spore-forming bacteria. Latent symptoms of *Clostridium difficile* infection (CDI) often mimic some flu-like symptoms. It releases toxins that cause bloating and diarrhea, with abdominal pain, which may become severe.

The colitis is thought to occur when this bacteria replaces normal gut flora that has been compromised, usually following antibiotic treatment for an unrelated infection. The disturbance of normal healthy bacteria may provide *C. difficile* an opportunity to overrun the intestinal microbiome.

From this brief description one can imagine that it may have first appeared that my daughter had the flu when she fell ill. It's now evident that the antibiotic treatment she was subjected to only exacerbated her condition. We also now know that the endoscopy they gave her released the toxins further throughout her bloodstream and contributed to her death.

So I finally got my answer, but not a release from the pain in my heart. I did get my Ph.D., however, in microbiology and continued to study the properties of these bacteria.

I went on to discover *Clostridium difficile* bacterium found in salads and new ways of how the fatal *difficile* bacteria are transferred from animals to humans in Scotland. In further studies I also discovered a new type of *difficile* bacteria in the intestines of cats and undertook genetic research on the clostridium bacteria in collaboration with Scotland Central Laboratory.

It was too late for our daughter when in June 2008, however, the headlines in the Scottish newspaper read:

> **An outbreak of *Clostridium difficile* (*C. difficile*) in a Scottish hospital is causing concern despite claims from health authorities that the outbreak is under control.**
>
> **...A ward has now been closed to new patients after a new case of the *C. difficile* bug was reported in the Glasgow hospital; four patients at the Victoria Infirmary have now tested positive for the infection...**

In discovering the bacterium, I made a difference, but a difference was also made in me.

Life Must Go On

Zaki and I returned to Jazan and went on to have four boys— we had so many children because we were hoping to have another little girl, but sadly that never happened. With Yazan (13), Yad (10), Malad (3) our family is almost whole but we will forever miss our daughter Asser. Whenever I see girls who are the age she would be now, or who are the age she was, my heart sighs.

Nevertheless, I am very happy to be around so many young women now in my capacity as Dean of Female Students at Jazan University. It was a surprise to be appointed to this position; I hadn't sought it out, but a great thing happened when almost ten years ago King Abdullah visited Jazan and upon seeing its conditions vowed to revitalize the region and to support the establishment of Jazan University as well.

A word about the development of Jazan is important because its development will lead to jobs and our university is helping women to prepare to be employed. In brief, after King Abdullah's initial visit, he visited again in 2013 and as a result he urged Saudi Aramco to complete the first phase of infrastructure projects for Jazan Economic City in order to attract investment and boost the region's development. This was a major turning point for the city. As a result Saudi Aramco, the largest investor in Jazan Economic City (JEC), is currently building a major oil refinery and electricity plant and is developing plans to develop the city.

The establishment of Jazan University (JU) in 2006 was intended as a significant step to provide the local communities in Jazan Province with educational opportunities with a modern touch, and up-to-date programs using the state-of the-art educational technologies. After King Abdullah's visit to the region in 2013 even more emphasis was placed on supporting the university and to positioning it to play a key role in the commitment of Saudi Arabia to a broad-based transition into a knowledge-based economy, based on demand for scientific research and education.

This is where I entered the story. Though I hadn't study management or administration, at 30 years old I had already proven my scientific prowess and had published a number of papers in peer reviewed journals. Two of my papers, for instance, came to the attention of the leaders. These papers included: "The Gulf Woman: Present Routes and Future Gates" and "An Introduction to the Science of Medical Microbiology." What the leaders realized through my work is that I was living proof of what they want for the society: Young, smart, and well educated women who can make a contribution not only to the Kingdom of Saudi Arabia but also to the world. I suppose that for this reason I was selected to receive the "11th Middle East Prize."

Dr. Marwah Bakri is awarded 11th Middle East Prize

On the occasion of the International Women's Day, Dr. Marwah Mohamed Hamoud Bakri, Dean of Female Students Academic Complex, was awarded the 11th Middle East Prize granted by the Middle East Excellence Award Institute of Datamatix. This award is annually bestowed upon pioneering leaders worldwide. Dr. Bakri is to receive the prestigious Award of Excellence on March 7th, 2012 in an official ceremony in Dubai, UAE.

The ceremony, which is scheduled in the Khalifa Tower, will be attended by high ranking regional and international VIPs. High profile guests include

Albert Al Gore, former US Vice-President, Dominique de Villepin, former French Prime Minister, a number of royal princes, sheikhs, and executive directors of internationally-renown scientific institutions.

Dr. Bakri has won the award for her excellence in leadership and decision making. She was nominated by experts and specialists in the Middle East using the international criteria of leadership.

His Excellency Professor Mohamed Bin Ali Al-Hyaz'e, the University Rector, congratulated Dr. Marwah for being awarded this prestigious prize, asserting that honouring Dr. Marwah is an honour for Jazan University and all its affiliated members. It reflects the honouring of Saudi women in general, to acknowledge her distinctive role in building the family and the society, and in contributing effectively in construction and development of this blessed homeland. This award was very timely since Saudi Arabia has provided women a better atmosphere for innovation and scientific development especially under the umbrella of excellent strategy for learning and higher education instilled and implemented by the wise leadership of King Abdulla Bin Abdul Aziz, Custodian of the Two Holy Mosques.

I was happy when I received this award, not only for myself and our daughter's memory, but for my dear mother who encouraged me and knew one day that I would arrive. It was also, in my eyes, a tribute to my husband who has been my constant partner and supporter since high school and to my father who equally supported my goals and made my husband promise to allow me to continue in my studies.

In my current capacity as the Dean of Female Students I have an unprecedented opportunity to help pave the way for other young women. A key part of my role and responsibility is to help inspire our female students to realize their dreams, just like I achieved mine. I can show them firsthand through my own experience that dedication and perseverance pay off and most importantly, I can relate to them and them to me. After all, I'm still not much older than many of them. I empathize with them and they know that and call me the "Dean of Hearts." In them I see my own daughter and whereas I have lost her, I have gained 7,000 student daughters of Saudi Arabia who look up to me for inspiration and direction.

As an Administrator I now have a new field of learning to conquer. I'm concerned with day-to-day concerns of what it takes to ensure that the university provides students with what they need to excel. It takes academic directors being accountable and the establishment of systems and mechanisms to ensure that the students have a voice. It also takes vision and my vision for the women studying at Jazan University is for them to leverage their education to accomplish great things for themselves and for our economy. At present, we have four major departments: computer science, management, engineering and agriculture, and kindergarten education. In each of these fields of study there are many opportunities for discovery and innovation and for the adaption of these disciplines to meeting the needs in our community and society at large. I want to make sure that our students don't encounter roadblocks in their academic experience that thwart their possibility thinking and preparation.

Indeed, I love what I am doing at the university and my university family but on a personal level I haven't found the limits of what I can do. I keep pressing forward and branching out into new directions. A new frontier that I am pursuing and am really excited about is business ownership.

Pulling all the Pieces Together

I live in a city with special biological assets and flora and fauna; I am a biologist, and the city is on the upward trajectory and growing. Collectively, these are the ingredients for a wonderful business formula I realized.

Navigating the business licensing frontier in Saudi Arabia remains challenging, but I was never one for shirking a challenge.

I am in the process of establishing the first beauty center in Jazan. Not just any beauty center though, it will be a spa in 900 meters of space, which I have already leased, and it will sell my line of specially formulated spa treatments that I am compounding from local ingredients mixed with other exotic and luxurious ingredients.

Importantly, the name of the Spa is my daughter's name: Asser.

It's a fun and potentially lucrative endeavor. My best friend Aisha is my partner and interestingly the business is incorporated through her daughter who is the same age as my "Asser" would have been.

I blessed to have the love of my sister Maysoum and my brother Hamoud; and that of my wonderful four boys, and my beloved husband—all of whom I adore. I can honestly say I am happy but its happiness defined with an ever present tinge of sadness.

About
Dr. Asma Abdulaziz Abdullah AL-Sultan

Subspecialty Consultant in Pediatric Cardiology

King Fahad Medical City (KFMC)

Dr. Al-Sultan was born in Riyadh, Saudi Arabia in 1967. Her current position is in the Ministry of Health, King Fahad Medical City (KFMC), Prince Salman Cardiac Centre, where she is a Subspecialty Consultant in Pediatric Cardiology; it is a position that has required many years of academic preparation, specialty training, and research.

Dr. Al-Sultan completed one year of training in Fetal Cardiology at the Rush Center for Congenital Heart Disease at Rush University Medical Center, Chicago, Illinois in the United States in 2014. Previously, from 2012 to 2014, she also completed two years of training in Non-invasive Pediatric Cardiology at the Rush Center. She passed the final clinical/oral examination in Pediatric Cardiology in Riyadh, Saudi Arabia in 2012 and was awarded the Saudi Fellowship in Pediatric Cardiology.

In addition to her qualifications as a medical doctor, she also obtained a Masters of Public Health from the University of Pittsburgh in the U.S. in 1999. A continuous learner, Dr. Al-Sultan has taken extensive training in her field. Prior to serving in her current capacity, she spent time at Harvard University's Medical School in 2014, where she was an observer in the Echocardiography laboratory. She was also a Research Scholar at Rush University and formerly worked with the Saudi Arabian Ministry of Defense and Aviation, in the Medical Services Department, where she was a Fellow Pediatric Cardiologist from 2009 to 2012.

A prolific writer and researcher, Dr. Al-Sultan has also authored many papers on topics in her field and has participated in numerous workshops and symposia.

Dr. A-l Sultan is an active member of the American Society of Echocardiography and of the Saudi Pediatric and Heart Associations.

She was selected by the Saudi Board Training Committee as the best "Senior Board Resident" for the year 2004 in Children's Hospital, King Fahad Medical City, and has also been recognized by the King Fahad Medical City for making valuable contributions to the Children's Summer Health Program that was held at KFMC. ❧

Dr. Asma Al-Sultan

Pediatric Cardiologist

"A Dream, Hope, and a Letter"

Early Life

My life started out unremarkably. I wasn't from a well to-do family and, as was common at the time, my mother wasn't educated. My father wasn't highly educated either but he was a deep thinker and an excellent writer. Importantly, he was my soulmate and source of inspiration from the start.

As far back as I can remember I had only one dream: to become a doctor and not just any doctor; I wanted to be a Cardiologist. I don't actually recall why I felt that being a doctor was my life's calling but somehow I never wavered from that dream. Even when I was hosted as a fifth grade student on a local TV show and was asked what I wanted to become when I grew up, I immediately answered without any hesitation that I wanted to be a Pediatric Cardiologist.

In the Saudi education system at the time in 1986, one's grades, as opposed to test scores, determined acceptance into medical school. Fortunately, with an average of over 90 percent I qualified straight out of high school for medical school admission. Acceptance was not automatic, however, and we waited anxiously each day for an announcement to appear in the newspaper that would show who had been accepted. My father was even more anxious than I was. When the announcement came, showing that I had been accepted, my father was overjoyed. He was my greatest supporter.

The letter my father wrote to me upon my acceptance remains one of the greatest inspirations in my life. In essence, he let me know that he was committed to me and my success and would leave no stone unturned to support me in any way. My father's support gave me the strength I needed to power myself through the very difficult and long learning journey ahead.

A Journey of a 1,000 Miles Begins with a Single Step

In retrospect, going directly into medical school out of high school was not preferable. While students were then able to take a full year's study in biology, chemistry, physics and math before concentrating on courses in medicine, it's not enough. Students need more time and more preparation. Furthermore, having to read and master high level science in a foreign language is very difficult. It took three months of dedicated and intensive study of the English language before I could really dig in, but even then it was hard to master the material. The subjects are tough and I really struggled to get through it; I survived only by digging in deeply with everything I had. Many students didn't make it and dropped out or changed their majors. But I stuck it out and didn't quit, and the experience transformed me and made me a fighter.

I imagine it must have been very difficult to be among the first Saudi women to study medicine. Even though I wasn't in this first group, it was no less difficult for me because of communication barriers and the lack of group discussion. The school faculty was predominately male, which inhibited our interactions. We female students did not feel comfortable conferring with either our male professors or our male colleagues about course material or lectures. In addition, the Internet and social media communication options available for students nowadays were not available during my years at college. Had I had access to the Internet it would have made studying a lot easier.

An additional challenge for me was not having any family members in the medical field. I had to figure out everything on my own. One thing I did have, however, was my father's love and support; it gave me the inspiration and encouragement to fight my way through.

A Father's Encouragement Makes All the Difference

For many people in Saudi Arabia, the main concern about women studying medicine is that it would place them in close proximity to men. An even greater concern is that in order to practice medicine a woman would have to work in a mixed gender organization like a hospital. My father let me know, however, that he trusted me and wasn't worried about such things. He didn't know, and neither did I, that one day I would willingly wear my veil while practicing medicine in a mixed gender environment.

Today, I wear my veil whenever I am in public in Saudi Arabia, including when I meet with my clients. I do this not because anyone makes me; rather, it's entirely my choice. I wear it because I want to and because it accords with my own beliefs.

While many in society were concerned about women studying medicine for the reasons mentioned above, my father was ahead of his time in encouraging me to become a medical doctor. In fact, he was so supportive that he even encouraged me to study abroad. To prepare myself for this possibility, I elected to study German in my first year of college.

The fact that I'd be blazing new trails and achieving something that no one else in the family had achieved motivated me to work really hard.

Just because you study hard doesn't mean you will make it. Indeed, I was nervous nearly the whole way through medical school and it wasn't until I was in my fourth year that I knew I'd make it after all. Essentially, I had learned how to teach myself, how to understand English and basically how to succeed.

Free At Last

I ultimately relinquished my fear of failure and freed myself. I was in my fifth year of university when this new reality sunk in. It was also at this point that I was finally free to marry. It was an arranged marriage but we had the choice to accept or decline the arrangement. My future husband and I sat down and negotiated our future. Importantly, we agreed to respect each other and each other's career paths. It was a good match and I can honestly say that my husband has become the other powerful source of inspiration in my life. He is 100 percent behind everything I do.

As we began our life together I had my first child after my graduation in 1995 and four months later I joined my husband in Pittsburgh, Pennsylvania, where he was admitted into the University of Pittsburgh to study for his Ph.D. in Public Health. We often talked about our professional interests and pursuits and, as a result, I too became interested in the public health field. With my son still in diapers and having gotten bitten by the learning bug, I decided to pursue a master's degree in Public Health while we were still in Pittsburgh. Over the next four years, I had two more sons and completed by master's degree. My husband also succeeded in obtaining his doctorate in 1999.

After returning to Saudi Arabia, my goal was to complete my residency program in Pediatrics. This took another four years, and as had become a pattern in my life, I had another two children by the time I graduated. The pattern was ingrained: Degree, baby, degree, baby…and now it was time to obtain another degree and go back to university one last time. This time, I specialized in Pediatric Cardiology, my profession today. While studying, I had had another child and shortly thereafter traveled back to the U.S. for two more years to subspecialize in Fetal Cardiology.

Finally, I have settled into my profession at the King Fahad Medical City (KFMC) in Riyadh, which incidentally is where my husband also currently works. Prior to joining KFMC, my husband had worked for two decades as an associate professor at local universities and training institutes in the Kingdom.

Heart and Soul

Working with children with heart problems is not easy. I feel the pain of their parent's grief, and it's especially painful when you uncover heart problems in the womb. It is my job in such circumstances to help the parents understand what's ahead of them. I am glad to say, however, that I have helped many parents understand that such a diagnosis is not the end of the world; there's hope and, in some cases, there are also interventions to help hope along.

Finding solutions to complex problems requires an all hands on deck approach. This means gleaning the most you can from your colleagues, no matter what their

gender may be. It's surprising that it's only now that I have allowed myself to cross the male-female barrier to interact with male colleagues to discuss work matters and to seek their counsel. I could have always done this, and I could have conferred with male colleagues at university but it was my own conservative nature that prevented me from doing it all of these years. I am over that now. Colleagues, I have come to realize, must confer in order to learn from each other.

I still believe, however, that there are valid reasons to be conservative in Saudi Arabia. We live communally, and what we do as individuals impacts our whole community. For instance, my husband's family as well as my own are very conservative. It is for this reason that I go the extra mile to ensure that everything I do and the way I do it brings pride to the whole extended family. Wearing my veil is a show of respect to all of our ancestors – but it's not a requirement imposed by my husband or by anybody else. This is what outsiders often don't understand; I am, in fact, free to choose.

Dreams Can Come True

My dream came true. Not only did I become a Cardiologist, but I also got to combine my love of children with my profession by specializing in Pediatric Cardiology. I am also proud of myself for overcoming all of the challenges I faced, including my own fears.

One of the biggest challenges I have faced is knowing how to strike the right balance amongst my duties as a mother, wife and professional. As women in the Arab world, and especially in Gulf societies, we are expected to safeguard our family life first and foremost, and we carry most of the responsibilities on our shoulders to accomplish this.

It's extremely important as professional women to ensure that our husbands do not feel slighted because their wives do not stay at home like most Saudi women. It's difficult for us as professional women in Saudi Arabia because in order to work we need more cooperation and assistance inside the home and outside of it as well. Existing laws, regulations and institutions impose barriers for women who work outside the home and in a professional capacity.

Another challenge I faced is that I had to study in Chicago, Illinois in the United States while taking care of my six children without the presence of my husband, in order to train in my subspecialty for two years. At that time, some of my children were teenagers attending high school and my youngest was at daycare. In addition to the usual day-to-day burden of raising and looking after my children, I had to manage their exposure to a different educational system and to different social norms. This required a great deal of time and understanding, while I was in the process of learning a new field. Despite the challenges, I was ultimately successful and my family had a positive experience overall. Looking back on that time, I feel proud of the way I raised them and that my investment in them has paid off.

The Road Ahead

Professionally, I remain ambitious and hardworking. I am constantly searching for new inroads and areas in which to prove myself and to succeed. I plan to continue my quest for knowledge and to enhance my research and analytical skills. My goal is to make a contribution to the advancement of knowledge in the fields of Pediatric Cardiology and Fetal Echocardiography.

Socially, one of the causes I am working on is establishing a support group for mothers of children with heart defects. These mothers are very scared and overwhelmed, and they need help and training in how to cope with their children's illnesses. Along these lines, I also intend to get involved with national health campaigns to educate our communities about health and wellness issues.

Upon reflection, my life's journey thus far has taught me an invaluable lesson: don't let the fear of failure stop you from trying. And, as the old adage goes: "If at first you don't succeed, try, try again."

Success is attainable. I am living proof of that. I now know that growth and fear go hand in hand; it's part of a package and if we fail to embrace the whole package, we will fail.

With six children, I have a large stake in the future. My main task as far as they are concerned is to be a good role model and to help them successfully navigate the world. For instance, we can't keep the Internet out but what we can do is effectively communicate our value system and encourage and incentivize them to act within it. I'm proud to say that a few of my kids have said that they want to become a doctor like me, but I'm just as proud of my two little ones who want to grow up to be soccer players.

The future is bright, in my view, and in my small way, I do what I can to make a contribution to ensure that it is.

About
Omaima Abdullah Al-Khamis

Omaima Abdullah Al-Khamis (أميمة الخميس) is a Saudi writer born in Riyadh. She obtained a B.A. in Arabic Literature from King Saud University in 1989. She later obtained a Diploma in English Language from the University of Washington in 1992, and a Diploma of Education from Faculty of Education in the year 2000. In 2009, she became a Certified International Trainer.

She has published a number of short stories, novels, and children's books, and has won the Abha Prize for story writing in 2001. Her work has been translated into English and Italian. Omaima has had weekly articles in the *Al-Yaum* newspaper, *Al-Riyadh* newspaper, *Al-Jazirah* newspaper, and the *Gulf Times* newspaper; she currently writes an article three times a week in *Al-Riyadh* newspaper under the title: *The logic of the clouds*.

She was formerly the Director of Educational Information in the Ministry of Education. She has also taught many courses in administrative, media and creative writing.

To promote cultural awareness, Omaima has convened cultural lectures inside and outside the Kingdom of Saudi Arabia. She also continues to offer courses and workshops in creative writing.

She is a member of the Board of Directors of the National Committee to raise awareness of Alzheimer's disease

She is a married mother of two sons and a daughter. ❧

Omaima Al-Khamis

Novelist/ Author

"The Logic of the Clouds"

Clouds are interesting; they conjure up different images and meanings to people at different times. On the positive side, clouds are sometimes considered as symbols of Divine presence...as they float in the atmosphere high above the ground. Conversely, as the sun disappears behind the clouds they may at times also be referred to as metaphors for doom and gloom.

I choose to view life positively and think about clouds as a metaphor for change, which is why I have named my weekly news program "The Logic of the Clouds."

My father with the Late King Abdullah

Clouds have their own internal workings; we can't control them, just as we often can't control how or when change happens.

In Saudi Arabia, change is happening and the signs are positive. With the focal point on youth, it is their hopes and dreams that matter most.

I remember the first time I went on the air for a television interview. I had decided that I would lift my veil but I was concerned about how my children would view this action and how they would be impacted by it. I didn't want them to be chastised at school or bullied about it. So, before the interview, I went to them to seek their views and gauge their reactions, bracing for the worst. To my surprise, they said: "Mommy, this is great. Do it!" I was shocked and further surprised that they asked their friends to watch me on the air as well.

I realized at that moment that although I couldn't see how the change was happening, it was happening in our society every day, especially through the youth - whether we knew it or not. Again, I think about the cloud metaphor because clouds are complex and formed by things intertwined underneath them and above them. Our youth are like the cumuliform clouds forming in the lower level of the sphere; they matter and have their own impact.

Change, like clouds, is the result of many pressures - some from the inside and some from the outside. These pressures have resulted in monumental changes in our society that are clear for all to see. Consider, for instance, that less than half a century ago it would have been virtually unheard of to utter a woman's full name in public. Women at that time were not just hidden under a veil; their entire lives and the way they lived it were concealed behind walls. Women didn't have a voice, a face, or the legal standing to act alone or independently in many regards.

It was this state of affairs that my mother, a Lebanese Palestinian, encountered in the 1960s when she married my father, a Saudi. She had been raised in Lebanon, attended an international school and graduated from university. When she met and fell in love with my father and moved to Saudi Arabia, it was a shock and a situation that required her to change her entire life.

Though she was a university graduate, she was not allowed at that time to work in Saudi Arabia. In fact, she would never be allowed to do or be anything again without the explicit approval of her husband and her husband's society.

In spite of such restrictions, women like my mother are among those who helped usher change into our society in their own subtle ways. My mother, like other women who moved into Saudi Arabia from more advanced Middle Eastern countries at the time, was a change agent within her home rather than outside of it. She ensured that her children, including her daughters, valued education and became learned individuals. There were books everywhere in our house, which was uncommon at that time. My siblings and I were encouraged to read them and to dialogue and debate with my mother about them.

Given our family's focus on education, I always knew that I would attend university and that it was the path for me to become whole. My mother even encouraged me to attend university before getting married, which was a radical point of view at the time as well.

I clung to my mother and incorporated her beliefs and values into my own. My relationship with my father, by contrast, was a bit distant and formal. I only interacted with him at dinner because he was a very busy and important man. As a writer, historian, geographer, statesman, and the founder of Al-Jazirah newspaper, he was in great demand.

We knew our father was famous but, as a child, when you see your father quoted in the newspaper, you just take it for granted and figure that it's commonplace. We didn't know what fame was and it didn't matter to us.

What mattered to me was my love for the written word. I always knew I wanted to be a writer. When I was six years old, I wrote something and showed it to my dad and he said: "You didn't write that did you?" My feelings were hurt. They were hurt further when he went on to say, "Don't focus on being a writer; just focus on your studies and do well in school."

I don't know why he said that. I didn't like it though and I didn't show him anything else I wrote for many years.

When I was a teenager he took us to Taif, a town near Mecca, where he attended a learning institute. When he showed us the institute, I could see that he felt emotional about it. Upon seeing him in an emotional state, which was unusual, I decided to write a story about what I imagined he was feeling and I showed it to him. He liked it, and it was the first time we made a positive connection about my writing.

My father was a scholar and a poet, but that's not what made me want to be a poet; it was just in me. It was something I couldn't ignore, something I couldn't resist; it was like noise coming from the depths of my heart.

I first began to write poetry in my early childhood but I quickly realized that it was not viable pursuit in a male dominated society that didn't want women to express their inner feelings. After all, poetry is about looking inward and, when expressed, it would expose the inner world of a veiled girl – and nobody wanted that, of course.

I discovered a trick, however, for getting my poetic thoughts out there. I began to weave my poetry into my short stories, which provided a way to hide behind the voices in the stories and, in the process, I became a prolific short story writer.

After having written ten books of short stories, I was finally ready for my grand symphony: my first novel. I did it and now I have three novels to my credit, one of which was even nominated for the Arabic novel prize. I'm also proud to say that my novels have multiple editions. It goes to show what's possible when one is driven and takes the time to discover alternative pathways for accomplishing one's goals. In my case, I found the way to get my poetic musings out there: I cleverly incorporated them into my novels without causing a storm.

After 20 years of an unpleasant experience working for the Ministry of Education, which was a dreary, gloomy, uninspiring place, I quit and dedicated myself to writing a novel about it. It was entitled: "Past, Singularity, and Masculine." To me, this says it all.

Writing has always been my true passion so I was very happy to join the Al Jazirah newspaper as a writer. Unfortunately, I was taunted by the claims that I only got the job because my father was the newspaper's founder and that he had actually written my work for me. This was an untenable situation, so I moved on to work for another newspaper where my voice was not questioned as being my own.

Today, in addition to writing for the newspaper, I also regularly tweet because that is the way that I connect with the young people. I usually tweet a few lines from my newspaper headlines and have found that it connects me well with the youth.

When I've been asked if I feel free, my answer is: Yes, I do feel free because, through my writing, I'm free to let my mind take me on my journeys. And, importantly, my spirit is free.

I do wear a veil, but not because I have to. I wear it to be a part of the culture because, to me, culture is about the traditions and this just happens to be one of them.

There is no need to get hung up on it; no one is forcing me to wear it – and certainly not my husband. We freely chose each other, which admittedly was out of the norm 23 years ago. From the very beginning, we understood each other's dreams and supported each other. He is a medical doctor and works with women and fully accepts women in the work place. Likewise, in my profession, I occasionally interface with men, which is not a problem for my husband. Fortunately, to be honest, we have a lot of help at home so I am free to work in my home office without the pressure of rushing to the kitchen to make dinner.

When I imagine the future of Saudi Arabia and the place for women in it, I recognize that I can't predict its rate or direction of change, but I do know that change is inevitable. I also know that women are playing a role in making change happen. As my mother's example showed me, women have the power to use the home as a testing ground for ushering in small changes, one at a time. Women are also instrumental in helping to instill values into the youth, such as inspiring them to acquire knowledge so that they

My beloved family

can leverage it to become positive forces for change. Increasingly, some women in our society are also being given the chance to formally become change agents, such as the women who have been appointed to the Shura Council and those that have been permitted to practice law, among others.

As for myself, when people come up to me and say, "Hey, your article made me think about something," "it gave me new point of view," or "your article changed my mind about something," I know that I have made a positive contribution toward changing our society.

In fact, if you ask me to define success for myself or for my two boys and daughter, I'd say we would be successful if we are able to add something to society that positively impacts it. My children will carve out their own paths and I will advise them as my mother advised me: "Be all that you can be; make a difference." My children are already making a difference, starting with the difference they made in me. The gardens of their young vivid imaginations, for instance, inspired me to write ten children stories that were subsequently published.

Do I want Saudi Arabia to change drastically overnight? No. It's my country, my home and it's where my memories are and where my family and friends are. I don't need it to be another country overnight.

There are certain things in the West I admire such as freedom of speech, respect for the constitution, and above all: Equality under the law. Seemingly, in the west there are few special privileges accorded to individuals; rather, it's about merit and being a citizen. I love that, and I also love my country, my home.

Afterword

There is no doubt the pendulum is swinging for Saudi Arabian women, as the stories featured in this book demonstrate. Saudi women are being educated at the highest levels and are increasingly seizing the opportunity to contribute in meaningful ways to medicine, science, law and other fields. Women are increasingly stepping out of their traditional roles and speaking up in unprecedented ways, such as being advocates for the environment.

With the passing of King Abdullah, who ushered in many new opportunities for Saudi women, some have questioned whether the pendulum will continue to swing in a positive direction for women.

Norah Al-Faiz, the highest ranking female ever in the government, was recently relieved from her position as Vice Minister in the education ministry, prompting many inside and outside of the Kingdom to wonder if this was an indication that advances for Saudi women would be rolled back. Indeed, constraints on Saudi women remain, evident in restrictions on women drivers and female athletes.

Collectively, the burning question is: to what extent can change for women be expected within Saudi Arabia in the near term?

The short answer is that time will tell. There are reasons for optimism as we observe Saudi women making great strides. While we were only able to feature a few of their success stories, we know there are many other examples of Saudi women who are successful and breaking new ground. The following offers a few additional snapshots of some of those stories.

Her Royal Highness Princess Lamia Bint Majid Al Saud. As the Executive Manager of Public Relations and Media of Al Waleed Bin Talal Foundation, she is an example of a modern day princess who is not content merely to sit back and enjoy her privilege. Rather, she is on a mission to do good and meaningful work.

"There are many stereotypes about Saudi women that need to be dispelled," says Her Royal Highness, "such as Saudi women are pampered." To the contrary, many Saudi women - even princesses - are working women these days. HRH is an example of the latter.

Educated in Egypt, she puts her degree in journalism to good use professionally not only her current senior position with the foundation but earlier with her own magazine, "Mada," and her book, *Sons and Blood*, published in 2011. She is also a businesswoman who established and ran three companies prior to joining the Al-Waleed Foundation.

When speaking with Princess Lamia, it was clear that she believes that women's progress in the workplace does not mean those same women wish to abandon their traditions. The obsession of people in the west about whether Saudi women can drive, she offered as example, "is ridiculous." Change happens incrementally as the different parts of society adjust, which, she added, is only natural.

Saudi women are happy and "whole" for the most part, she noted, and what makes them "whole" is their love for their families and community, and embrace of their culture and traditions. For instance, many - like herself - see their parents every day and typically have big family gatherings on Fridays. One cherished tradition in her family is going into the desert and communing under tents. Princess Lamia said she draws inspiration from her mother, who completed high school when the princess was 11 years old. Her Egyptian-born mother always told her that "nothing was impossible."

Reflecting Saudi religious values and cultural norms, Princess Lamia also underscored the importance of giving back and, in this spirit, has adopted two children. She knows firsthand the many good things that are happening for Saudi women and expressed her hope that western media would pay more attention to these things.

Dr. Entissar Al Suhaibani, Associate Professor of Genetics. As a scientist, Dr. Al Suhaibani knows that breakthroughs are possible and that you can't precisely predict when and where they will happen. This is true in the social realm as well. As a scientist, she has been able to cross social and professional barriers.

For instance, she works late in a laboratory without being questioned and often confers with male colleagues. She has also traveled to other countries such as Korea and India, which enriched her understanding about scientific matters and about other people.

Her travel to Korea was particularly enlightening. Like Saudi Arabia, Korea is in the midst of experiencing and accommodating massive and rapid technological change – but has also managed to hold onto the essence of its culture. In her view, Korea is a great model for Saudi Arabia to emulate.

According to Dr. Al Suhaibani, managing change from a societal point of view requires the right balance between technological development and social development. Saudi Arabia has absorbed technological change at lightning speed but the next frontier encompasses other aspects of human development. "We need more museums, more orchestras, and more theaters; not just places to shop," she observed. "In other words, we need to develop all facets of our humanity and to raise it up to even higher levels."

As a scientist in the genetics field, she has given a lot of thought to how things change, and why. It's not surprising, then, that her thoughts have turned to imaging how societal change occurs and to what extent and in what time frame society can absorb change.

Dr. Al Suhaibani studies the impact of radiation on the human genetic structure, which has led her to ponder at what point might radiation cause the genetic code to change?

Social and professional issues are intertwined and impact one another, Dr. Al Suhaibani noted. "As female scientists we have to design our work around our limitations so that it can be accomplished in the female section, but in our cleverness, we are sometimes able to find work-arounds. For instance, when we work in hospitals women and men are able to work side by side therefore we look for opportunities to do so."

Dr. Al Suhaibani shared deeper insights into her thinking, as follows:

> ...Frankly, my big dream is for our society to evolve to the point that scientists could have joint research centers and openly collaborate with each other as male and female counterparts. As for myself, I want to work late; I don't want to quit working at 4pm, which I'm now required to do.

> I also dream that the walls between the university and the community will be removed one day. Let's leverage each other; let the community in and let us go out into the community.

> Isolation is neither good nor possible, ultimately. With globalization we can't keep the world or change out - it's coming in no matter what. Sometimes I think that we think that we are special because we are Saudis. When I go out of the country and see other Saudis who stand out, I can imagine how special we can feel but at the same time I see other people looking at us with disdain. There is a wide gap between how we see ourselves and how other people see us. From the perspective of my discipline, while there are undoubtedly differences between people, we are all humans and the same deep down. I do think we are special as Saudis, in many respects, but to the extent that this is so I feel that we have a special obligation to perform well and in special ways. If we can't prove that we are special by our performance, then we are not.

> On balance, in many ways, I think that ours is a society catching up with itself and the times and with all of the changes that have been imposed internally and externally. Being concerned with the rate of change of things, I can understand that changes have been very rapid in our society on the one hand and slow in other regards. For instance, when I joined university there not many students studying science in Saudi Arabia and of these, only a few were females. Today, seven years later, there are many.

Less than four decades ago when I was born in 1969, for instance, it was not typical for women to be educated so my mother, like many others at the time, was only educated through primary school. My father, however, was one of the first university graduates in Saudi Arabia.

He was educated in Islamic studies and later taught in Yemen and the United Arab Emirates. Fortunately, as a child we got to travel with him and perhaps through that experience a seed was planted in me for the love of travel.

Traveling had a transformative impact on my father as well. He spent time in Lebanon, when it was known as "Paris of the Middle East," and perhaps because of his exposure to that society he believed in the equality of the sexes. He also had a camera, which was very unusual, and played records at home—which was even more extraordinary. Our library at home was perhaps our greatest worldly possession and it was through my love of reading the books in our library that I began to imagine what I might be when I grew up. I also imagined other people's lives and felt connected to the world through my reading. I couldn't wait to travel to experience things I imagined and to see other people and the way they lived. I felt hemmed in by all of the rules of our society.

I was lucky. My father encouraged my dreams and higher level educational pursuits, which just less than ten years ago was considered exceptional. His support was essential because I knew from the very beginning that education was a route to freedom and I wanted to be free.

I was lucky again when the person with whom I was matched for marriage was actually a good match, but I did not accept him sight unseen—which was seen as being radical at the time. I insisted that my future husband travel from Jeddah so that I could meet him first. We had a heart to heart talk and I told him two important things about myself and we made our deal. Today, we are happy and have three children, one girl and two boys. My husband, who is an Industrial Engineer, does not get in the way of my professional pursuits and has given me permission to travel, though admittedly he worries when I visit nuclear plants.

What I have learned, on balance, is that some breakthroughs are small and some are big but collectively and incrementally they all matter. Little by little I hope that I, my family and my society continue to break through to the next level of peace, happiness, enlightenment and contribution.

Dr. Monera Alalola, Former Deputy in TVTC for Women. Dr. Alalola was one of the first students enrolled in the first school in Riyadh for girls in 1961, and was the second person in the Kingdom to obtain a Ph.D. in Linguistics. She has dedicated her life to training females and never married. She began her career at Prince Nora University in Riyadh in 1975, where she worked for 32 years until she retired in 2014 as Deputy Governor of the Technical and Vocational Training Center (TVTC).

As head of the first vocational college for females and aware that vocational training is designed to meet the needs of the economy, Dr. Alalola always kept abreast of the latest economic developments in the Kingdom and their impact on the demand for women in the work place.

While the gender segregation in work places and in schools limited opportunities for women, it also created demand and arguments in favor of women entering new disciplines, such as computer science. As Dr. Alalola explained, "What if a computer breaks down in a work place for women, isn't it better for women to be qualified to fix them?"

Dr. Alalola has been a long standing advocate for expanding opportunities for women in the workplace and for broadening the list of license categories for women. Computer science technicians, beauticians, fashion designers and even electricians are now among the vocations in which women can be licensed. In 2015, there are 18 vocational training centers in 18 regions. Entrepreneurship training is one field that is on the rise, Dr. Alalola noted, "especially as there are fewer opportunities for employment and therefore women must be trained and encouraged to go into business for themselves." Looking back on her life's work, she said she is pleased because she now sees many trainers who are Saudi trained through the vocational centers she oversaw and who are now training others. Such signposts are very positive for the role of women, she said, and for their prospects of broadening their participation in the economy.

Sara Al Omari, Licensed Lawyer. Sara was in the first graduating class of female lawyers and was one of the first among four females to pass the bar. She is 28 years old, unmarried, and lives in Jeddah. Her brother is a businessman and she originally wanted to follow in his footsteps but after taking one law course, she was hooked even though, at the time, there was no prospect of a Saudi women being able to practice law. Miraculously, things changed rapidly and by the time she completed her studies, women were permitted to sit for the exam and become licensed attorneys. Her concerns today are perhaps similar to those of any lawyer, male or female, and include how to manage a work-life balance. Like other lawyers, she typically works late into the night and harnesses technology to keep in communication with clients and colleagues. She sees the future as bright for upcoming Saudi female lawyers and, as more women are able to intern in law firms, they will increasingly be prepared to establish their own law practices one day. Sara is one of the first lawyers who joined Banyan Mohmoud Al-Zahran in her female-owned law firm.

Asma Al-Dowaian, Principal of Al Ebtikar School and Businesswoman. Born in 1970, she is the mother of seven children and has been married for 25 years. She graduated in 2003 with a degree in English Literature from King Saud University at a time when there were few available professional options for women. Having lived in the U.S. from the age of three until she was eight, with English as her first language, she had the option of becoming a translator - but she rejected that.

In reflecting on her journey up to this point, she recalled that when she returned to Saudi Arabia, she couldn't speak Arabic and faced culture shock. In particular, she was struck by what she considered harsh treatment of children, a practice she challenged by establishing her own elementary school.

There were other cultural traditions, she recognized, that had to be accepted. For instance, hers was a traditional marriage and, as was the tradition, she did not meet her spouse before their wedding. It was a difficult adjustment to live with a man she did not know and she missed her family. Her mother, however, helped smooth the way with frequent visits and by checking in on her.

Asma was in her first year of college when she got married. Altogether, she said it took about one year to adjust to her new life, but appreciates that she was lucky because her husband was not a difficult man, like perhaps some others. This made the adjustment easier and she fully bonded with her husband. By the time she graduated from college, she had her first child and other children soon followed, but that didn't stop her from working.

She worked at the Ministry of Education for six years before she and her husband established Al Ebtikar School, which she has run and operated for 14 years. Her concerns center on her work both as an entrepreneur and as principal of the school she founded. She is focused on developing the best elementary school curriculum, recruiting and maintaining the best teachers, and other workplace issues. Long gone are any questions and concerns about adjusting to Saudi traditions; she embraces them fully.

When asked her opinion about the rate of change for Saudi women in the society, she lamented that things are changing too fast. "Women should obey their husbands," she underscored. One of the worse things in the society, she said, is that more and more couples are divorcing, which negatively impacts the children. She believes the formula for Saudi women's success is for to remain true to their purpose, which is to bring love and affection into the home and community, to sacrifice themselves for the family and the greater good of the society by being obedient wives, and to abide by the Holy Quran. This does not mean that women can't work or make professional strides but they also must be sure to maintain the right balance between home and work, she advised. Adhering to this formula does not mean rejecting all of modernity. Children, for instance, must be allowed to use the Internet, she said, but when they do use it they must be supervised and guided by their parents.

In Asma's view, success is not measured individually but is instead measured in terms of the happiness of not only her entire family but also that of her extended family and community.

The short profiles of the women above provide further insights into the thinking and accomplishments of some Saudi professional women. There are many others to mention, such as Dr. Huda Al–Mansour, who is a scientist and inventor with numerous patents in her area of specialization of blood diseases and Thalassemia.

Indeed, there are many women to watch in Saudi Arabia who are on the move and who are making great contributions for their society and the world.

C

CREATIVE